Weighing up the Evidence

TIMELINE:

Ireland

Annabel Wigner

Dryad Press Limited London

Contents

D4401

J/941.5

Typeset by Tek-Art Ltd, Kent
and printed in Great Britain by
Anchor Brendon Ltd
Tiptree, Essex
for the Publishers
Dryad Press Limited,
8 Cavendish Square,
London W1M 0AJ

ISBN 0 8521 9716 0

ACKNOWLEDGMENTS

The author and publishers thank the following for their kind permission to reproduce copyright illustrations: BBC Hulton Picture Library, pages 18, 44, 47, 52, 60, 61; Bord Fáilte (Irish Tourist Board), page 8; Commissioners of Public Works, Ireland, page 5; Edimedia, page 29; Imperial War Museum, London, page 49; Mansell Collection, pages 9, 19, 36; The Tate Gallery, London, page 14; the Board of Trinity College, Dublin, page 10; *The Ulster Star*, page 57. The map on page 53 was drawn by R.F. Brien.

Cover illustrations: *Top:* Allihies, Beara Peninsula (Bord Fáilte); *Below left:* Security forces in action, Belfast, 1981 (Topham); *Below centre:* Boy and girl at Cahera, during the famine (Mansell Collection); *Below right:* 12 July marchers (Topham).

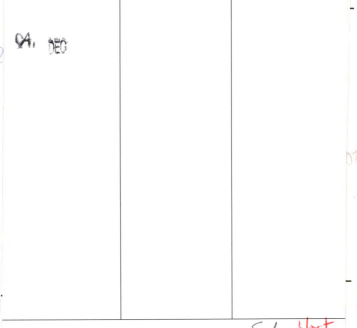

An Introduction to Two Nations

The historical background to modern twentieth-century Anglo-Irish politics is a stormy and confusing story. Those involved in the present-day relations find it difficult to make decisions which will have support from all the different groups of people who make up Irish society. While politicians representing all dimensions of opinion discuss constitutional change, many lives are being lost, and the violence continues to grow both in Northern Ireland and in mainland Britain.

There are two "Irelands". One is Ulster, or Northern Ireland, and this area of land is ruled directly by the Westminster Parliament of Great Britain. The larger of the two Irelands is Eire, the Independent Republic, which some British people incorrectly call Southern Ireland. There is no constitutional link between Eire and Great Britain. All previous ties between the two nations were removed, and were finally dissolved when the Republic of Eire came into existence in 1949. For British people it is the link with *Northern* Ireland, or Ulster, which plays such an important part in current politics.

Because of the past connection between Britain and Ireland, it is impossible to write a history of Ireland which does not include a great deal about Britain's involvement in Irish affairs. The first chapter of this book examines traditional Gaelic society. It is important to realize that Ireland had a distinctly separate culture. However, Ireland's problem has always been its closeness to the English coast. The later chapters tell the story of how Britain became involved in Ireland through war and colonization. Ireland was part of the British Empire and today Ulster remains one of the oldest surviving examples of English conquest and colonization.

Written and visual evidence from many different sources is included throughout this book. It shows how there are many conflicting viewpoints in Irish history. Since all evidence is biased, it is important to understand how to interpret it. This is not an easy skill to acquire. It is necessary to read widely, and to discuss issues with different people.

One thing you will notice in the sources is anti-Irish prejudice. It is clear that anti-Irish humour is considered acceptable in almost every form. This is one example of bias, and you should bear it in mind when you weigh up the evidence.

As this is a short chronological survey, much detail has had to be omitted. It is hoped that this outline will be sufficient to encourage you to read more widely on areas which you find of particular interest.

A study of Anglo-Irish relations is of great benefit to all those who are interested in history. Events considered of national and international significance in British affairs changed the path of Irish history. The problems facing all the people of Ireland today have their roots in Britain's imperial past and should not be ignored. The dilemmas surrounding constitutional change in Northern Ireland provide us with an example of the way our lives are affected by our past. Studying history should also teach us how people learn to develop relationships with each other. The Anglo-Irish relationship has always proved too difficult for most politicians to handle. There are three nations to consider, and strongly held opinions prevent political agreement. It would seem essential that all those involved in the continuing disputes should learn to understand the others' points of view. It is hoped that this book can help towards some understanding, if not a satisfactory conclusion. A history which is being written while events are still taking place can only present the facts as clearly as possible, and allow the reader to judge the future outcome.

The Land, The People

PEOPLE ON THE MOVE

On modern maps, boundary lines separate one nation from another. The names of modern countries relate to different political units. However, long before nations and political identities stabilized in Europe, Scandinavia, Britain and Ireland, people moved across great expanses of this land – they migrated.

EARLY SETTLERS IN IRELAND, c. 7000 BC

The oldest human remains discovered in Ireland date settlement to 7000 BC: they show that nomadic tribesmen used stone implements for hunting and fishing. However, little is known of how these people organized their societies. It was they who introduced the custom of burial chambers, one of which has been dated by radiocarbon techniques to before 3000 BC. Other evidence of their lifestyle includes pendants, bone pins and pottery.

Eventually these people gave up nomadic life and settled in simple farming communities. The only evidence we have of these is the remains of their "everyday rubbish". This shows that there were a few isolated settlements in central Ireland, but that many more communities decided to live on the northern and eastern coasts.

3000 BC

It was not until the Ice Age had finally retreated that the early settlers were able to build permanent settlements in Ireland. Other migrants joined their communities, and introduced more sophisticated farming ideas. They were herders of animals as well as crop farmers, and they lived in houses made of stone, earth and wood. The most impressive examples of their way of life are the burial chambers and the stone tables, or Dolmens, which mark the graves of their Kings. The passage grave of Newgrange in Ireland predates others in Egypt, at the temple of Abu Simbel, and in Crete, at the treasury of Artreus, but these later examples are far more famous than the ones found in Ireland. It is only recently that the evidence of settlement in Ireland has been examined thoroughly.

Two kinds of grave have been discovered. Court graves were often marked by a mound, raised by three large stones which were then covered with earth. Today, many mounds remain without the covering of earth, and so we can see how they were made. The dead were placed with all their possessions, in long galleries underneath the mounds. Passage graves were even more complex, and some are very large indeed. Long passages led into a burial chamber which held the ashes and possessions of the dead. Newgrange burial chamber, in the valley of the River Boyne, is one of the largest to have been found in Ireland.

At Newgrange, the rising sun travels along the passageway, which is sixty-two feet long, and hits the centre of the tomb for seventeen minutes on the shortest day of the year. This may have had special religious meaning. It tells us that the people who built the grave had a quite sophisticated understanding of the movement of the sun. To honour their

This is a photograph of the Newgrange Burial Chamber in County Meath. A carved stone could be moved across the entrance, and the grave is approached by a long passageway. Round-bottomed pots, stone axes and tools of flint were placed with the dead.

dead they decorated the tombs with patterns. In the photograph of the Newgrange burial chamber you can see that these patterns are spirals. When you look at other artefacts of early Irish society, see if you can see more spiral patterns.

IRELAND'S YEARS OF GOLD, 3000 BC

Four thousand years ago, Ireland was famous for the export both of raw gold and of finished products of gold. The craftsmen in gold would have lived in settlements of very simple huts made of wattle and daub, but the skills they used in their metalwork were extremely complex.

Although no gold deposits survive today, there must have been a surplus of gold at this time, if the people of Ireland were able to export it. They imported tin, amber and jet.

Gold was used for personal adornment. Apart from for jewellery, in what other ways could gold be used as a status symbol?

IRELAND AND THE GAELS

Gold and bronze were eventually replaced by the use of iron, which was introduced into Ireland by the Celts. It has proved impossible to date the Celts' arrival with accuracy, but they were certainly established in Ireland by 500 BC. Their descendants became known as the Gaels.

Celtic tribes settled in all parts of Europe, and in many places they were assimilated into the Roman Empire. However, this was not the case for Ireland. Ireland may have received visitors from Rome, but the Romans never came as conquerors. Therefore, when the Roman Empire fell, Ireland remained untouched. The Gaelic culture that was established over this period was able to develop a unique style. Later, nationalists would refer to the Gaels as an example of an Irish culture unaffected by developments caused by the English connection.

GAELIC SOCIETY

The Gaelic Celts called their land Erin. There are some descriptions of their society in Roman histories, but no eyewitness records of their lifestyle were written until the Catholic Church had established itself in Ireland and made a study of Gaelic society. Until this happened the Gaels told the stories of famous people to each other, and these were passed on from one generation to the next. This is how history was first collected. Going so far back in time gives us problems in sorting out historical fact from myths or legends.

Eventually, the stories, or sagas, were collected together and written down in Gaelic. From these sagas we are able to learn about the organization of Gaelic society, as well as reading about Irish heroes such as Cuchulain and the Fenian leader Finn MacCool. The sagas are a combination of poetry and historical details. They were told by shanachies or story-tellers, who were considered very important in Gaelic society.

In Gaelic society people were seen as belonging to one of three groups. The "aristocrats" included tribal kings, warriors, druids, judges (called Brehons), poets and historians. The freemen were merchants and farmers. And the slaves were prisoners-of-war and usually few in number. At various times strong leaders emerged, but the Gaels were not unified politically. Nonetheless they did have a common culture and social system, and they all spoke the same language — which is an important force in bringing groups of people together.

A Gaelic landowner:

This description of a Gaelic landowner includes the number of houses he owned, the furnishings and possessions inside and outside his houses.

He is a man of three snouts:
The snout of a rooting boar that cleaves dishonour in every season,
The snout of a flitch of bacon on the hook,
The snout of a plough under the ground;
so that he is capable of receiving a king or a bishop or a scholar
or a brehon from the road, prepared for the arrival of any guest
company. . . .
He has a bronze cauldron in which there is room for a boar.
He possesses a green in which there are always sheep without having to change pasture.
He and his wife have four suits of clothes.

(*Source:* quoted in *The Course of Irish History*, edited by T.W. Moody and F.X. Martin, Mercier Press, 1967)

The number of animals owned by a person or a kinship group was an indication of wealth. Here a snout, or nose, of an animal gives us a guidance to the value of this man's property. He is considered to be an honourable man, whose house has food, and whose land produces crops.

Gaelic society stresses the importance of scholarship and the law. Would a landowner today welcome "a king or a bishop or a scholar or a brehon from the road" in the same way?

Gaelic society was organized into a series of clans, each of which occupied and possessed a particular territory. Having an ancestry within a clan was very important, as legal rights to property, for instance, could be established without question, if lineage (or ancestry) could be traced within the clan. The clan organized both property and legal matters, but did not deal with family matters as such.

Family ties within the clan were complex. There was an extended family group, and children were often fostered. Parents were not expected to marry and stay together in the way we would expect today, and a family included three generations, rather than just the small unit of a mother and a father and at least one child. All children were looked after, whether they were fostered or of the original family group, and parents and grandparents were respected equally. This family system kept relationships peaceful within the clan itself, and the fostering system often prevented wars between different clans.

Although Gaelic society was strictly organized and hierarchical, all were equal and no-one was above the law. The laws were named after the judges, or Brehons, who studied and interpreted the law. Their judgements were handed down in oral tradition and became accepted.

The Brehon Laws safeguarded the traditions of the Gaels and were applied within each clan. They covered every aspect of life, from the duties and responsibilities of the privileged to family relationships. In matters of crime and injury, equality and honour, the laws were based on the principle of compensation. For example, if a murder had been committed the victim's family was entitled to claim a sum of money for the loss. This system of compensation was complex. Capital punishment was rarely used.

Gaelic farmers cultivated land, but ordinary people tended to live a nomadic life, herding cattle. Wealth in each clan was judged by the number of cattle owned. The number of fields under arable cultivation was therefore small, and milk products such as butter, buttermilk and sour curds formed the staple diet, with oat cakes which were "griddled" with butter. Ale was also made from oats, or from rye. The pastoral life of the Gaels did not encourage communities to build permanent living places. Many of the people, from a wide social range, lived in small huts, sometimes within fortified hill settlements.

The Gaels elected a High King to rule them. Each tribal king ruled a *tuatha*, which was the name given by the Gaels to their political units. In special ceremonies each Gaelic King was "wedded" to the land he ruled. If he wished to stand as a candidate for High Kingship he had to break his vows, and give up his titles to other land. High Kingship was considered sacred, and a candidate would be selected only if he was considered to be morally and physically pure. If the tribal kings decided on one candidate, he left his tribal lands and moved to the headquarters of the High Kings of Ireland. This was Tara.

Cormac Mac Airt, High King of Tara:

Beautiful was the appearance of Cormac in that assembly, flowing and slightly curling was his golden hair. A red buckler with stars and animals of gold and fastenings of silver upon him. A crimson cloak in wide descending folds around him, fastened at his neck with precious stones.

Tara was a strongly fortified hill settlement, built at the centre of an ancient road system. It was a scholastic and religious centre as well as a meeting place for assemblies of clans, and was used for games and horse-racing and martial trials.

A torque [a thick twisted necklace] of gold around his neck. A white shirt with a full collar and intertwined with red gold thread upon him. A girdle of gold, inlaid with precious stones, was around him. Two wonderful shoes of gold, with golden hoops upon his feet. Two spears with golden sockets in his hands, with many rivets of red bronze. And he was himself, besides, symmetrical and beautiful of form, without blemish or reproach.

(*Source:* from a translation by Douglas Hyde, *The Faber Book of Irish Verse*, Faber & Faber, 1978)

If you read this extract aloud, you will find it has a special rhythm. It has many beautiful images. Do you think that this description was first produced as oral history, or as written history? How reliable is this source as evidence to the historian?

THE SECOND AGE OF GOLD

Historians have called the Bronze Age Ireland's First Age of Gold, and the flowering of Christianity in Ireland, the Second Age of Gold. Christianity arrived in Ireland with St Patrick in 432 AD. Gaelic customs and practices were strongly established and so he devised a new missionary approach. Druids, Brehons and shanachies were respected people whose love of learning, history and law gave Christians a base from which to set up informal monastic systems. The Church did not attempt to undermine or change Gaelic law and customs. It did not interfere with inheritance practices or communal ownership of property, and did not force the Gaels to marry or give up adopting or fostering children. Strict celibacy was not customary in Gaelic society, and divorce was easily obtained. The Church did not approve of this, but thought it wiser not to interfere, and the new religious community was accepted into the society of the Gaels. When Rome was over-run by German tribes, and Christian Europe collapsed, Ireland remained isolated. Gaelic society kept Christianity alive and preserved its own traditions as well.

Another famous Irish Christian, St Columba (534-97) wanted the

Christian communities in Ireland to have their own copies of religious texts. He thought that having more Christian texts would encourage the Gaels to adopt Christianity more seriously and give the religious communities more status.

The Book of Kells, from which this is a page, is the most famous example in Ireland of a religious manuscript. It was produced by three monks at about the end of the eighth century. Each page was painstakingly copied, and the text was given beauty by illumination. The Book of Kells is as much a work of art as a copy of a religious text, and the illustrations reflect the highly individual skills of the monks who worked as artists and writers. They would have considered their work a very special way of praising God.

The flourishing side by side of the Christian and the Gaelic communities represents the height of the "Golden Age" of Ireland. In metalwork, for instance, the ideas and skills of the two groups combined to produce work of even greater beauty than before. It is to this time that modern-day nationalists return in their search for an ancestral identity.

VIKING RAIDS

From 795 AD, Vikings attacked Ireland, England and mainland Europe. Eventually they settled, intermarried, traded and became Christians. Not all the Irish liked the Viking presence in their homeland, and a member of the Munster royal family challenged their authority. Brian Boru was ruler of Munster, and became High King of Ireland in 1002. He united the Irish chieftains against the Vikings, and defeated them. For a short time the whole land of Ireland was under his control, but in 1014 he was killed at the Battle of Clontarf. The Vikings were able to take control once more, although they were never so powerful again.

IRELAND AND THE NORMANS

The Norman invasion of England in 1066 was to lead to a great change in Irish society. The change was gradual, as only small numbers of Norman knights at first journeyed from Wales to Ireland. One powerful Norman, the Earl of Pembroke, became involved in Irish affairs in the Kingdom of Leinster, and the Normans were able to win because they had superior weapons. The English King, Henry II was determined to force the Earl into submission, because he was far too powerful in Ireland. By 1171 the Earl of Pembroke had given homage to the English King, and in theory at least, England ruled three quarters of Ireland and castles and walled towns were erected. The Normans settled in Ireland and began to practise Gaelic ways. These settlers were known as the "Old English".

By 1204 Dublin Castle was built. In later years this was to be the centre of British administration in Ireland. In 1297 an Irish Parliament was opened, and the ruling classes of Ireland were invited to attend. Three years later, towns and boroughs sent their representatives there also. To prevent Gaelic habits growing in the Norman community the Statutes of Kilkenny were passed by the ruling Normans in Ireland in 1366. Intermarriage was forbidden, as were the Gaelic language and Irish harp music. The "Old English" were regarded with distrust by England.

 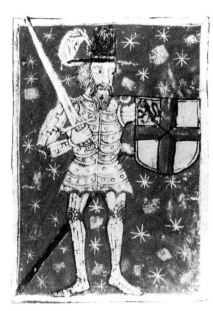

Before and after: a Norman view of a Norman settler. What is shown as having happened to the Norman knight? Is this a sympathetic viewpoint?

ON REFLECTION:

Think carefully about why people migrate. What reasons have been given in this chapter to explain settlement in Ireland?

For many years Gaelic society and the Catholic Church flourished together in the communities in Ireland. Which of these two influences would have more power and control over the lives of ordinary people?

The Rule of the Tudors

WHO RULED IRELAND?

When Henry VII became the first of the Tudor monarchs in 1485, he inherited little in Ireland that seemed to be of obvious benefit to him. As tradition demanded, he claimed, as King of England, to be "Lord of All Ireland", but he was able to claim kingship over only the small area of land around Dublin, known as the English "pale". In effect, political power in Ireland was wielded by powerful Gaelic and Norman leaders who lived in strongly fortified castles and were in absolute control of the land they owned, and of the people who lived on it. In their own way, they were the direct rulers of the people of Ireland, and a change of monarch in England did not pose much of a threat to their power and local supremacy.

During the Tudor period the Irish Parliament began to consist of only English representatives. In 1494 Poyning's Law brought the Irish Parliament under English control: no laws could be passed without the consent of the Privy Council in England. This was the beginning of the centralization of power in England.

By the Act of Supremacy in 1534, Henry VIII made himself Supreme Head of the Church in England. He had split the country away from the Catholic Church and papal authority, in order to free himself of a wife and enforce his power as monarch. The Act was introduced into Ireland in 1536, but little religious change occurred. Henry did not introduce Protestantism into England and Ireland, although his descendants were able to make use of his act to plant it in Ireland at a later date.

THE KILDARE REBELLION

The most powerful of the Irish lords was the Earl of Kildare, whose family claimed the right to the title of Lord Deputy in Ireland. The Kildares led a rebellion against Henry VII in 1494, and in 1537 they rebelled again. Henry VIII moved with ruthless aggression against the leaders, who were executed for crimes against the English State. Lord Offaly, or "Silken Thomas", as he was called in Ireland, had appealed to the Pope for help in the rebellion and this was a treasonable act. Ireland was now associated with a foreign power and this was seen as a threat to English State security. From this time onwards, Ireland, rebellion and treason were linked in the minds of English monarchs.

NEW LAWS PASSED BY HENRY VIII . . . ON INHERITANCE

The English King passed two new laws in 1541. One made him King of Ireland. The other introduced changes in the laws of inheritance. Under the Brehon Laws, property in Ireland was owned by everyone jointly, and everyone stood as equal in a society which was Gaelic in origin. Inheritance of property and status did not follow the English rule of primogeniture.

This is how the English system of inheritance worked in practice with the royal family.

The following extract from a sixteenth-century History of Ireland describes how leadership of the *tuatha*, or basic political unit, was inherited.

How was inheritance different in Ireland?

The inheritance descendeth not to the son, but to the brother, nephew or cousin . . . for the child being often times . . . young and unskilful, were never able to defend his patrimony, being his no longer than he can hold it by force of arms. But by that time he grow to a competent age, and have buried an uncle or two, he also taketh his turn, and leaveth it in like order to his posterity.

(*Source:* Edmund Campion's History of Ireland, quoted in *Irish History from Contemporary Sources 1509-1610*, Constantia Maxwell, Allen and Unwin, 1923)

To the English legal mind the Gaelic system seemed disorganized and primitive. The Irish people were regarded as barbarians by the English, and the customs of their society were criticized.

The new law on inheritance, passed in 1541, was called the Law of Surrender and Regrant. Under this law, all those who owned land in Ireland surrendered it to Henry VIII. If a former landowner paid homage to the English Crown, his land would be returned to him, and a title would be created for him which would be inherited thereafter according to the English system of primogeniture. If an Irish lord rebelled, the land would be taken away and re-distributed amongst other loyal subjects. This divided Irish society and undermined Brehon Law, causing customs which had been in use for hundreds of years to disappear. Irish leaders did not understand at first how the new law could be applied against both them and their families. It appealed to the ambition of powerful Irish families who saw none of the risk involved in the process of surrendering their land, but only the gains that would be made through the connection with the English monarch. England was thus able to extend its authority.

. . . ON APPEARANCES

Laws on the Statute Books in England stated which fabrics and furs could be worn by different groups of people. Rich merchants, for instance, could not wear the aristocratic cloth of gold. The following is an extract from a law made in 1536, which affected people in Ireland:

This engraving, produced in 1521, shows the three types of Irish soldiers – horsemen, kerne and gallowglass. The horsemen carried a javelin, the kerne a sword, bow and arrows, and the gallowglass a special long-handled axe. Some of the kerne were called "wood kerne" or bandits. The gallowglass were Scottish or Scandinavian mercenaries.

Henry VIII's Act of the English Order, Habit and Language, 1536:

... no person or persons ... shall be shorn, or shaven above the ears, or use the wearing of hair upon their heads, like unto long locks ... or have or use any hair growing upon their upper lips ... or use or wear any shirt, smock or kerchief ... coloured or dyed with saffron ... and that also no woman use or wear any [skirt] or coat [or ornaments] ... after the Irish fashion.

(*Source:* quoted in *Landlord or Tenant? A View of Irish History*, by Magnus Magnusson, Bodley Head, 1978)

Look back at the picture of the Norman knight at the end of the last chapter. What can you see in that picture that is forbidden by this new law?

The saffron robes, and the long forelocks grown to hide the faces of warriors from their enemies, were distinguishing features of Gaelic soldiers. Why has the law made special mention of these two details?

EUROPEAN ATTITUDES TO THE GAELS

Contemporary accounts of Tudor Ireland praise the landscape, but find little to say that is positive about the people. During the reign of Elizabeth, Spain played a part in Irish resistance, and one Spaniard, Captain Cuellar, wrote of his travels in Connacht and Ulster, and of the Spanish Armada. His attitude to the Gaels is typical of most Europeans of this period.

The custom of these savages is to live as the brute beasts among the mountains.... The most of the women are very beautiful, but badly

This portrait is of Sir Henry Lee of Ireland. It was painted in 1594 by Marcus Gheeraerts, who was a court painter in the reign of Elizabeth I. He specialized in full-length portraits and painted many famous Elizabethans. This portrait is now in the Tate Gallery. Sir Henry Lee married an Irishwoman. In this painting he has paid a great compliment to her. He has chosen to be painted as a Captain of the woodkerne.

dressed. They do not wear more than a chemise, and a blanket, with which they cover themselves, and a linen cloth, much doubled, over the head, and tied in front. They are great workers and housekeepers after their fashion.

(*Source: Captain Cuellar's Adventures in Connacht and Ulster, with Captain Cuellar's Narrative of the Spanish Armada and his adventures in Ireland*, written in 1589, translated by R. Crawford, published by Elliot Stock, 1897)

THE TUDOR REGIME IS ENFORCED

The Statutes of Kilkenny had forbidden the wearing of traditional Irish dress and intermarriage, but the new law of 1536 went further. The lawgivers, poets and harpists of Gaelic society were banned and could be found guilty of treason if they kept traditional customs alive through oral history, poetry and music. Use of the Gaelic language was forbidden.

Some other minor changes occurred after Henry VIII's death. Under his son, Edward, the English Book of Common Prayer was introduced and the Catholic mass was banned. Under his daughter, Queen Mary, there were some experiments in settling groups of English people in particular parts of Ireland. However, neither of these measures was successful, because English administration in Ireland was not able to enforce them. The greatest changes took place during the reign of Henry VIII's second daughter, Elizabeth I.

ELIZABETH I, QUEEN OF ENGLAND

Elizabeth had much to prove as ruler. Henry had divorced Catherine of Aragon, to marry Anne Boleyn, and Elizabeth was the daughter of this new marriage. In the view of Roman Catholics, Elizabeth was not the legitimate heir to the throne, as Anne Boleyn had not been Henry VIII's true wife. Elizabeth had been brought up as a Protestant, but she did not believe in making extreme changes in the laws relating to religion. The Act of Supremacy passed by Henry VIII was confirmed, and English Catholics were compelled to pay a fine if they would not attend Protestant services. Elizabeth's religious settlement did pacify the people of England, and English Catholics were able to enjoy religious freedom and fulfil civil duties. It was not until the 1580s that difficulties abroad began to affect England's attitude towards Catholic powers, and this was to influence Irish affairs and Catholics in both England and Ireland.

ENGLAND AND SPAIN

The most powerful country in the European world was Spain. The Spanish King controlled an enormous empire and was also the most important Catholic King in Europe. When the Pope excommunicated Queen Elizabeth in 1570, declared her a heretic, and called for her assassination, King Philip of Spain could not ignore him. Catholic priests were being smuggled into England to attempt the reconversion of England to Catholicism, and Philip also gave his support to Elizabeth's Catholic rival, Mary, Queen of Scots, who was a prisoner in England. It is against a background of England's mounting fear of Catholicism, and hatred of the power of Spain, that events in Ireland should be judged.

ELIZABETH AND THE IRISH LORDS

Elizabethans knew little about Ireland, and Elizabeth's Council never constructed a clear and decisive policy for dealing with it, but one thing was clear: Spain would be able to invade England by using Ireland as a starting point of rebellion. There were no reliable maps of Ireland and it seemed a confusing space of unknown territory, inhabited by people whose way of life was totally different from that of the English. Elizabeth never went to Ireland, but she had her first experience of a Gaelic chieftain in 1562.

A Gaelic chieftain in rebellion:

Shane O'Neill came to England to escape being captured by the English soldiers garrisoned in Ireland. His father had surrendered his land to Henry VIII and been given the English title of the Earl of Tyrone. He had then made his eldest son Matthew his heir, as was customary under English law. Shane O'Neill drew upon the support of his clan, imprisoned his father, and murdered Matthew. When it seemed that the English would capture him, he came to the court of Elizabeth to ask for pardon.

And now Shane O'Neill came from Ireland . . . with an escort of gallowglass, armed with battle axes, bare-headed, with flowing curls, yellow shirts dyed with saffron . . . large sleeves, short tunics and rough cloaks, whom the English followed with as much wonderment as if they had come from China or America.

(*Source:* William Camden's Royal History of England and Ireland, quoted in *Irish History from Contemporary Sources, 1509-1610*, edited by Constantia Maxwell, Allen and Unwin, 1923)

In what ways was Shane O'Neill defying English Law relating to Irish clothes?

Ireland is only a short distance from the shores of England. China and America are far away. Can you find reasons to explain why English knowledge of Ireland should be so limited?

After his spectacular entrance, O'Neill threw himself to the floor and spoke, at first in Gaelic, and then in English, of his right to inherit under Brehon Law. He then submitted to English rule.

WAR WITH IRELAND

Although they were aware that Ireland could be used by the Spanish as a starting-point for invasion, neither Elizabeth, nor her chief advisor Lord Burghley, wished to get involved in a war with Ireland. This would be too expensive and would have no immediate benefit. Fighting would be difficult on such treacherous terrain, and the Irish would be able to use guerilla tactics which would drain English resources. This was a familiar problem for England: weighing financial concerns against concerns about national security. However, in 1579 the English Queen had no choice but to fight Ireland, for the Irish rebelled and threw themselves into what seemed a major international crisis. Rumours and information gathered by English spies were telling of movements of Spanish troops in the Netherlands, a growth in the Spanish navy and a collection of munitions in Ireland. An attempted rebellion was defeated, and the Irish and their Spanish and papal supporters were executed.

By ancient right of chieftaincy, the Earl of Desmond claimed more than 800,000 acres of Southern Ireland, including 1550 square miles in Munster, Leinster and Connaught. He was much more powerful than any English Lord and, without question, the most powerful of the Irish leaders. The family had lost favour with Elizabeth as early as 1565, and when the last Earl was killed in 1583, the land was confiscated and divided up between English adventurers and entrepreneurs.

The geographical position of Munster made that province particularly vulnerable to Spanish influence. It was decided therefore that Munster would have to be completely conquered and a "plantation" of colonists firmly established. Large areas of land were given to Englishmen, who were then responsible for transporting English settlers to their new land. As a long-term strategy this was not successful, as not enough settlers applied to go. In the short term, the English invaded Ireland, on the grounds that it was necessary for English State security.

In 1580 the Pope offered protection to all who were prepared to fight Elizabeth. A Spanish invasion force was defeated in Ireland by English troops. To prevent this happening again, a new type of warfare was introduced.

The Massacre of Munster, 1580:

The English commanders in Ireland decided to make Munster a dead area. No person or animal was to be spared and the whole countryside was to be flattened. Munster was invaded during March, when traditionally the herds of cattle were moved on to the plains, and crops were just about to be sown. The people who survived the first massacres died of famine.

Edmund Spenser was a poet and courtier who went to Ireland as Secretary to the Lord Deputy. He acquired land in Ireland and wanted to settle there. After the execution of Desmond he was given 4,000 acres of land in Munster. He described Munster before and after the invasion:

> Sure it is . . . a most beautiful and sweet country as any is under heaven: seamed throughout with many goodly rivers, replenished with all sorts of fish . . . with goodly woods . . . good ports and havens opening upon England and Scotland, as inviting us to come to them.

> . . . that in short space . . . a most populous and plentiful country [was] suddenly left void of man and beast; yet, sure, in all that was there perished not many by the sword, but all by the extremity of famine which they themselves had wrought.

(*Source:* quoted in *Ireland under Elizabeth and James I*, edited by H. Morley, Routledge, 1890)

In what ways might Edmund Spenser's account be thought to be biased?

The English used a "scorched earth" policy because of difficult terrain, and the Irish advantage of using guerilla tactics. How would an Englishman like Spenser have justified the use of this method of warfare?

Martial law in Munster:

To quell resistance, Sir Humphrey Gilbert, Military Governor of Munster, ordered that

> . . . the heads of all those which were killed in the day should be cut off from their bodies and brought to the place where he encamped at night, and should there be laid on the ground by each side of the way leading into his own tent so none could come into his tent for any cause but commonly he must pass through a lane of heads.

(*Source:* from a diary written by Thomas Churchyard, eyewitness to the Munster slaughter, 1580, quoted in *Ireland: A History*, Robert Kee, Weidenfeld and Nicolson, 1980)

What feelings do you think developed between Irish people and English colonists as a result of this action?

The war in Ireland continued to drain the Royal Treasury, and it was some time before England could begin to compete with other European powers in political importance. In 1588, the threat of invasion and colonization was removed, when the Spanish Armada was defeated.

THE BEGINNING OF THE EMPIRE With the defeat of Spain, England was able to build an empire in Ireland, and extended this strategy westwards into the New World of America and the

Caribbean, and eastwards to India and Africa. Many Elizabethan soldiers and sailors used the experience they had gained in fighting in Ireland, in the newly discovered continent of America.

THE EARL OF TYRONE AND ELIZABETH I

A second plantation of Ulster was planned and put into action, and the Queen made it clear that every settler had to be English and Protestant. Ulster was to be a racially pure colony. Other Irish chieftains rose against the Tudor regime, the most successful being the Earl of Tyrone, who led a combined force of Irish and Spanish troops. Spain did not give enough help to Tyrone, and English troops defeated him in 1603.

Spanish hopes of invading England from Ireland were once again destroyed, and Philip's desire to control Protestantism was curtailed. This was less clear to contemporaries than to us, but Tyrone's defeat was regarded as a defeat of Spain as well.

THE DEATH OF QUEEN ELIZABETH

The death of the Queen followed a few hours after Tyrone's submission. Elizabeth was the first English monarch able to claim control of most of Ireland. The result was a legacy of bitterness and hatred which was to have a lasting effect on policy-making over the next three hundred years.

This seal shows Elizabeth Tudor, Queen of England, mounted on horseback, with rays of light streaming behind her. Crowns surmount the Tudor rose of England and the fleur de lis of France. The writing around the seal proclaims her Queen of England, France and Hibernia. The claim to Hibernia, or Ireland, marks a new dimension in Tudor administration, and Anglo-Irish relations.

ON REFLECTION:

Between 1560 and 1603, different groups of people migrated to Ireland. They became known as the "New English", and were drawn from all social classes. Some were looking for a career in politics; others were adventurers, soldiers and settlers. In what way would their attitudes towards the Gaelic Irish differ from those of the Old English?

The nature of the conflict in present-day Northern Ireland has its roots in the history of the sixteenth century. The English Reformation had little effect in Ireland, and Protestant settlers formed a religious minority. What effect would this have upon the development of a Protestant Irish culture?

What English laws had most effect on Irish society during the sixteenth and early seventeenth centuries?

Protestant Power and Politics

This woodcut by Albrecht Dürer was made in 1498, for a religious text entitled "The Apocalypse of St John". The "apocalypse" is the name given to the coming of the end of the world, which is described in the New Testament book of St John. Many people in Europe in the fifteenth century had believed that the end of the world might happen in 1500, and Dürer had this in mind when he produced this woodcut. He represents the end of the world as four horsemen of war, disease, famine and death. Some people hoped that 1500 would bring changes in the way people lived. What do you think Dürer wanted to change?

THE EFFECTS OF WAR

The wars that ravaged Ireland in the sixteenth and seventeenth centuries were no worse than others being fought on the European mainland. In all cases the people who suffered the greatest hardship were the peasants.

At the death of Elizabeth in 1603, large parts of Ireland lay in devastation. From the north, in Ulster, to Munster in the south, crops and buildings had been burned and destroyed, and farm animals lay slaughtered in the fields. Perhaps as many as 5,000 people lost their lives in Munster alone, during only one campaign. The slaughtered animals fed English soldiers, and thousands of cattle were deliberately burned to starve the Irish to death. Their bones remained bleaching in the sun for years afterwards.

And no spectacle was more frequent in the ditches of towns, and especially in wasted countries, than to see multitudes of these poor people with their mouths all coloured green by eating nettles, docks and all things they could rend above ground. These and very many lamentable effects followed their rebellion, and no doubt the rebels had been utterly destroyed by famine, had not a general peace shortly followed Tyrone's submission.

(*Source:* an eyewitness account written by John Moryson between 1602 and 1623, quoted in Richard Berleth, *The Twilight Lords*, Allen Lane, 1978)

The potato had been introduced into Ireland at this time. What would be the advantage of planting a root crop during a time of war?

Do you think that the effects of famine on this scale would have influenced the Earl of Tyrone's decision to surrender?

THE FLIGHT OF THE EARLS

After the submission of the Earl of Tyrone, English power began to expand in Ulster. Eventually, both Tyrone and his neighbour the Earl of Tyrconnell decided to leave their lands, taking their families with them, as English civil servants were taking control of the administration. Under the Law of Surrender and Regrant, these lands were now forfeit, and taken by the English Crown in 1607. The Earl of Tyrconnell died in 1607; the Earl of Tyrone lived on for another eight years. They were both buried in Rome.

COLONIZATION IN ULSTER, 1607

A substantial amount of land was left vacant for colonization, and it was in Ulster, which had been least affected by English administration, that another planned plantation went ahead. Geographically, Ulster had been cut off from most of the devastation caused by the Anglo-Irish wars, but now that the forfeit lands had no aristocratic tenants, the Crown was able to launch plans for another colony. From this time, English administrators were sent in on a permanent basis to carry out government policy in Ireland. Irish people were gradually excluded from these posts.

Can you see why Ireland was considered suitable for colonization?

Food is abundant, and the inhabitants eat and entertain very well . . . the usual drinks being Spanish wines, french claret, very good beer and excellent milk. Butter is used abundantly with all kinds of food. . . . There is also plenty of fruit – apples, pears, plums, artichokes. All eatables are cheap. A fat ox costs sixteen shillings, a sheep fifteen pence, a pair of capons, or fouls, five pence; eggs a farthing each, and other things in proportion. A good sized fish costs a penny, and they don't bother about selling game. They kill birds almost with sticks. Both salt and fresh water fish are cheap, abundant, and of excellent flavour.

(*Source:* from a letter of Dionysius Massari, the Papal Nuncio's Secretary, sent from Limerick to Florence in 1645, quoted in James Carty, *Ireland 1607-1782*, C.J. Fallon Ltd, 1949)

WHY COLONIZE?

Several Tudor and Stuart writers were interested in colonization strategies, and wrote articles and essays to interest people in settlement abroad. One of the incentives was the urge to depopulate England of its poor. In the case of Ireland, it was felt that a strongly committed Protestant plantation would overcome Catholicism eventually, by outbreeding the Irish. In his essay "Of Plantations", Sir Francis Bacon outlined the economic advantages:

Planting of countries is like planting of woods; for you must make account to leese almost twenty years profit, and expect your recompense in the end . . . the people wherewith you plant ought to be gardeners, ploughmen, labourers, smiths, carpenters, joiners, fishermen, fowlers, with some few apothecaries, surgeons, cooks and bakers. . . . In a country of plantation first look about, what kind of victual the country yields of itself to hand; . . . . Consider likewise what commodities the soil where the plantation is doth naturally yield, that they may some way help to defray the charge of the plantation.

(*Source:* Sir Francis Bacon, "Of Plantations" (Essay 3), written in the early seventeenth century)

PLANTATION SCHEMES

Two separate plantation schemes took place. From 1606 onwards, Scottish Protestants, called Presbyterians, settled in the eastern part of Ulster. From 1608, the City of London Merchants organized a colonizing programme for English Protestants to be settled in the northern part of Ulster. As the settlers moved into Ulster, the Irish were dispossessed, and were forced to move out into the hills and neighbouring countryside. Sometimes the Irish were encouraged to return as labourers and tenant farmers, to the land that had once been theirs. Large numbers of labourers were needed to clear the land and grow crops. Where this happened a tense situation developed between the two groups of people. In some areas there was no mixing of the communities at all.

As the British Empire expanded in the seventeenth century, Acts of Trade established which goods were to be produced by colonists for Britain. There were advantages and disadvantages to this system of economic control.

How would English people benefit from the labour of colonial settlers in Ireland?

Cheap labour was essential if the settlers were to survive economically. In America and the West Indies, black African slaves were used to produce sugar, cotton and tobacco. From which groups of Irish people would English settlers find labourers to work their fields?

A MASSACRE OF PROTESTANTS: THE KILKENNY UPRISING

The tension between the two communities erupted into violence in 1641. The Catholics turned on the Protestant settlers. A great deal of unrest had been created by the increasing restrictions on the practice of Catholicism and by the English administration of Ireland, as well as by the results of plantation settlement. The uprising was confined to Ulster because plans for an all-Ireland rebellion were betrayed.

The leaders of the Irish community did not expect their followers to massacre Protestants, but anger and bitterness had simmered for so long that the plantation communities were often the targets of brutal revenge. Protestant refugees flocked to Dublin. There was not enough food and shelter for so many people, and every building, outhouse and stable was full to overflowing. Some refugees lay in the streets.

I have known of some of them that lay almost naked, and having clothes sent, laid them by. . . . Others that would not stir to fetch themselves food. . . . And so even worn out with the misery of the journey and cruel usage, having their spirits spent, their bodies wasted, and their senses failing . . . very many of them died.

(*Source:* Sir John Temple's eyewitness account, 1641, quoted in James Hewitt, *Eyewitnesses to Ireland In Revolt*, Osprey Publishing Ltd, 1974)

Written descriptions like this were published in England, often with pictures drawn by English artists who had not been eyewitnesses to the events. Often the stories were exaggerated, and Protestant in bias. Why was this kind of propaganda issued by the English authorities?

What sort of details would an historian need to examine when weighing up the effect of this sort of literature?

PROTESTANT AND CATHOLIC HISTORIES

Many hundreds of people were killed in this uprising, but this is almost less important than the effect it had on the Protestants in Ireland. From this time two distinct communities – one Protestant and English, the other Catholic and Irish – can be said to have developed in Ulster. The separation of these two communities was reinforced by stories which became part of the oral and written history of the settlers. The division of the communities survives today.

THE IRON FIST OF CROMWELL'S ENGLAND

The 1641 crisis in Ireland came at a time of great unrest in England. Charles I and Parliament clashed over the way in which royal power could be used, and civil war broke out. In 1649 Charles I was executed, and the Stuart monarchy overthrown. European people were horrified. Fear spread through English Protestants that Royalist supporters would attempt to invade England, using Ireland as a base. The Irish Parliament resisted Republicanism and supported the monarchy. Oliver Cromwell was in charge of the army, and the leading force in the Republican government. He was a dedicated anti-Catholic and his foreign policy was particularly aimed against Spain and its imperial policy in the west.

CROMWELL AND IRELAND

Cromwell decided to deal with the threat of invasion by leading an army to Ireland in 1649, intending to subdue Catholic resistance and establish a Protestant regime. By his actions in Ireland he established an image of cruelty which has survived to the present day.

Cromwell remembered the massacres of the Protestants in 1641, and decided to wipe out Irish resistance in key areas. In order to prevent the outbreak of full-scale war, which would cost the lives of more English soldiers, he decided to make an example of some towns in Ireland. One of these was Drogheda, which had a population of three thousand people at this time. Cromwell wrote to the President of the State Council, John Bradshaw, in September 1649:

It has pleased God to bless our endeavours at Tredah [Drogheda]. . . . I believe we put to the sword the whole number of the defendants. I do not think thirty of the whole number escaped with their lives. Those that did, are in safe custody for Barbadoes. . . . And truly I believe that this bitterness will save much effusion of blood, through the goodness of God.

I wish that all honest hearts may give the glory of this to God alone, to whom indeed the praise of this mercy belongs. . . .
I rest,

Your most humble servant,
Oliver Cromwell.

(*Source:* quoted in James Carty, (ed.), *Ireland 1607-1782*, C.J. Fallon Ltd, 1949)

Cromwell used the threat of forced transportation to Barbados. What other group of people was being forcibly shipped to the West Indies at this time?

A new boundary line was devised. Catholic landowners, who held land on the east side of the river Shannon, were forced to give up their land and move west of the river. Their land was confiscated and redistributed to Protestants. By 1658, 80 per cent of Irish land was owned by Protestants. Irish tenants and labourers had new landowners, and were forced to remain under Protestant control. Catholic landowners who resisted this change faced the death penalty or slavery in the West Indies.

THE MONARCHY IS RESTORED

When Cromwell died in 1658, there was no-one who seemed able to provide strong leadership in his place. The Republican army feared a rebellion from within itself, or disturbances from radical working-class Protestants in England, and so a request was made for the restoration of the monarchy in 1660. Charles II sympathised with the cause of the Catholics; his brother, James, openly practised his Catholic faith. When James II took the English throne in 1688, Parliament feared the growth of a thoroughly Catholic court and administration, which would undermine their power. A suitable Protestant monarch was therefore found in the daughter of James II, who had married into the leading Dutch family. Both Mary and her husband, William of Orange, were Protestants. William demanded joint sovereignty, with his wife as Queen. Parliament agreed to this, and William invaded England.

With French money and troops, James II landed in Ireland, and found support from both Catholics and Protestants. Loyalty to the Crown, rather than to religion, gathered Irish people together. In 1689, Ulster was once again the centre of resistance, this time with a difference.

THE SIEGE OF DERRY

Confusion was felt throughout the areas of Protestant settlement, and rumours of Catholic massacres of Protestants spread like wildfire from town to town. King James ordered a new Catholic garrison to relieve the old one in Derry. The leading citizens did not wish to seem disloyal to the King, but thirteen young apprentices took a swift decision against the wishes of their elders. They slammed the gates of their city shut on 7 December 1688, shouting "No Surrender!" A red flag was raised as the siege began. James and his army were shut outside the city walls.

Alderman Norman and the rest of the graver citizens were under great disorder and consternation, and knew not what to resolve upon. One of the companies was already in view of the town and two of the officers within it, but the younger sort who are seldom so dilatory in their resolutions, got together, run in all haste to the main guard, snacht up the keys, and immediately shut up all the four gates and the magazine.

(*Source:* an account of the siege of London-Derry (1689) by the Reverend George Walker, quoted in James Carty (ed.), *Ireland 1607-1782*, C.J. Fallon Ltd, 1949)

The following extracts are from eyewitness accounts of the siege of Derry. James did not close in on Derry immediately and full siege conditions began only in April and were to last until July 1689.

... The Irish army appeared before our city, but at that distance that one of our cannons had enough to do to reach them; but in short time they approached nearer to our walls. In the first place we burned all our suburbs and hewed down all our brave orchards, making them about as plain as a bowling green.

Why did the people of Derry use a "scorched earth" policy as part of their defence of their city?

We have been surrounded in this poor city for divers months ... exposed to danger without ceasing or intermission. ... We have seen death in all its horrible shapes, and we are every moment entertained with spectacles of misery and mortality. Sickness and disease are entered within our gates, and pale famine is visible in every countenance. ...
One friend looks at another, and sees his misery, but cannot prevent a lingering death. ... We cannot refresh ourselves with such scraps and morsels as we formerly allow'd to our dogs. ... Nevertheless God has made us this day a defenced city and an iron pillar and brazen walls against the whole land.

(*Source:* a sermon preached by the Reverend Mr Sethwhittle, 1689, quoted in James Carty (ed.), *Ireland 1607-1782*, C.J. Fallon Ltd, 1949)

What do you think gave the people of Derry the will to survive the siege?

Conditions inside Derry were very difficult, and thousands died of starvation. William of Orange was not prepared to give the city immediate help, and it was some time before he gave orders to send in relief ships. Ships sailed up the river Foyle twice before daring to break the boom which had been set across the river. On 28 July the ships broke through with supplies, and the siege was broken.

THE DEFEAT OF THE JACOBITES

James was defeated in two further battles, at the Boyne and at Aughrim, and William of Orange won an important place in Protestant history. Every year history is re-enacted in Ulster with celebrations of the bravery of the Apprentice Boys and the Battle of the Boyne, although present-day emotions have little real foundation in the events of the seventeenth century. The celebrations take place on 12 July, and supporters of the "Orange" cause travel from all parts of Northern Ireland to join the Apprentice Boys' Parade in Derry. The route of the march traces the pattern of settlement of the seventeenth-century plantation, from the "Bogside" where the Catholic settlement was originally situated, to inside the walls where the Protestants were in the majority.

After his defeat, James returned to Europe. Although in exile he was still considered the monarch of Catholic Irishmen and women. Those who felt that they could no longer stay in Ireland went to Europe or America as soldiers or as settlers.

ON REFLECTION:

The Protestants who established themselves in sixteenth- and seventeenth-century Ireland believed they were "predestined" as God's chosen people. How would they justify their place in Irish society?

Naval and economic supremacy made possible the creation of the "First" British Empire. How significant a place did Ireland have within the Empire of this period?

Those who live in Derry today, and are Protestants, feel that they have a special right to belong to their homeland. What effect has the siege had on the history of the settlers there?

Geoffrey Keating's Forus Feasa, *written in 1632, was the first general history of Ireland to be published in the Gaelic language. Here is an extract from the translation:*

Anyone who sets out to trace the history . . . of a country should explain the condition of the country and of its people. Since I have undertaken to examine the origins of Irish history I cannot but deplore the prevailing anti-Irish bias. . .
This is illustrated by the works of Cambrensis, Spencer, Stanihurst, Hanmer, Camden, Barkley, Moryson, Davies, Campion and other British writers (since the Norman invasion). . . . .
I am old, and some of them were young. I have seen and understood the great historical books which they never saw. . . . And I have not been moved by love or hatred for one party or another.

(*Source:* quoted in James Carty (ed.), *Ireland 1607-1782*, C.J. Fallon Ltd, 1949)

Keating dates the anti-Irish writing in English from the time of the Norman invasion. Does the evidence presented in this book indicate that his viewpoint was correct?

What explanations does Keating give for the anti-Irish bias in English writing?

He writes that he has "not been moved by love or hatred for one party or another". (This means that he is unbiased.) Do you think that a writer of history can present an unbiased account?

How does an historian learn to detect bias in primary sources?

An Age of Change

THE PENAL LAWS

Between 1695 and 1725, those involved in governing England passed a series of strict Acts of Parliament. These were called the Penal Laws, and they restricted social and political freedom. In Ireland, the same laws were passed by the landowners who controlled the Irish Parliament, and they were enforced by those who ran the headquarters of British rule, Dublin Castle. "The Castle" became the symbol of Protestant rule and English ascendancy.

Under the Penal Laws, anyone in England or Ireland who was not a member of the Anglican, or established Church of England was not allowed to attend schools or universities, and could not take a job in politics, the civil service or any of the professions. All religious outsiders – including non-conformist settlers, such as the Presbyterians, as well as Catholics – could be persecuted.

In Ireland it was forbidden for the Catholic Church to appoint senior officials such as bishops, and churches were allowed to fall into ruins, because no money was allotted to preserving them. Catholics were forbidden to own land, and could not inherit it. The Gaelic language was allowed to fall into disuse, as English became the official language of Ireland, and children had to be taught in English. Gaelic traditions and dress began to disappear altogether, as the English administration grew stronger. Irish Catholics were allowed to practise their faith, and were able to keep alive this aspect of their lives. Often it was to their priests that they turned if they needed help, and so the priests became an inspiration in rebellion, and gave guidance and help in times of misery and hardship.

SOCIAL AND ECONOMIC DIFFERENCES IN IRELAND

Ireland was one of the countries on the itinerary of travellers who were making the "Grand Tour" of Europe. Few of the people who visited were uncritical, and many were appalled by what they saw. The income of Irish landowners ranged from £7,000 to £20,000 a year. There was a great gulf between the rich and the poor.

A land of freedom?:

To discover what the liberty of a people is, we must live among them, and not look for it in the statutes of the realm: the language of written law may be that of liberty, but the situation of the poor may speak no language but that of slavery.... The cottages of the Irish, which are all called cabbins, are the most miserable hovels that can well be conceived: they generally consist of only one room; mud kneaded with straw is the common material of the walls ... these are rarely above seven feet high ... they are about two feet thick, and have only a door which lets in light instead of a window.

(*Source:* Arthur Young, *A Tour in Ireland; with general observations on the present state of that kingdom made in the years 1776, 1777 and 1778, and brought down to the end of the year 1779,* London, 1780)

An illustration from Arthur Young's book. Irish people were often too poor to make improvements on their land. When they could afford to do so, they could get no additional reward for being good farmers. Many landlords offered no security of tenure to their tenants. They called them "tenants at will" and could evict them without notice. What effect would this have on farming?

A peasant's cottage:

Half a dozen children, almost naked, were sleeping on a little straw with a pig, a dog, a cat, a chicken and a duck. The poor woman spread a mat on a chest, the only piece of furniture in the house, and invited me to lie there. The animals saluted the first ray of the sun by their cries and began to look about for something to eat: . . . I got up very soon for fear of being devoured.

(*Source:* Le Chevalier de la Tocnaye, *A Frenchman's Walk through Ireland 1796-1797*)

In the eighteenth century most people earned their living from jobs relating to farming. The work was often seasonal. How would this affect family income?

Landlords often left their estates to overseers, and lived in England. How would this affect the conditions of work for the labourers?

LANDLORD AND TENANT

We are used to thinking of slavery in connection with the shipment of black African slaves to America. This mass migration of people reached its height at this time. Those who traded in African slaves, or bought them for their plantations, said that Africans were inferior because they were black, were pagans not Christians, and lived in simple agricultural communities. We understand that slavery is evil, but eighteenth-century people in Europe thought that they were superior, and wrote at length about this.

The following description of the treatment of Irish labourers is interesting because it is written by an Englishman who disapproves of what he witnesses in Ireland.

A landlord in Ireland can scarcely invent an order which a servant, labourer or cottier dares to refuse to execute. Disrespect . . . he may punish with his cane or horsewhip. . . . Landlords of consequence have assured me that many of their cottiers would think themselves honoured by having their wives or daughters sent for to the bed of their master, a mark of slavery that proves the oppression under which such people live.

(*Source:* Arthur Young, *A Tour in Ireland*)

Do you think that there are differences which should be taken into consideration, that separate the American and West Indian slave systems from the system of landholding in Ireland?

In Arthur Young's opinion, how is the treatment of women servants that much worse than the harsh treatment of the men? Do you agree with this viewpoint?

Those who worked the land as labourers in England and Ireland suffered the greatest poverty. Catholic tenants in Ireland were not allowed to pass on their rented land to just one of their descendants. When they died, their land had to be subdivided, and it became impossible for those who inherited the divisions of land to grow enough food to feed a family. The main crop they lived on was the potato. Once the potato crop had been planted and lifted, Irish labourers would go to England and find seasonal work to earn them extra money. Because they were used to extreme poverty, they took any job, no matter how low the wages. This caused unrest and race riots, one of which erupted in London in 1780.

MIGRATION   There was a steady flow of migration from Ireland, as conditions there were so appalling. Some tenant farmers moved permanently to London and Europe. Ever-increasing numbers settled in America.

REVOLUTION   As in England, political life in Ireland was led by rich Protestants. Groups of people who had influence created places in power for those who would follow them personally. Parliamentary parties did not exist as we know them today, and voting was based on a property qualification.

Working-class Protestants could be relied upon to support this system of power, because it upheld their religious beliefs. Catholics were excluded from politics altogether. This gave Protestants a sense of security and resulted in a belief that Irish Anglicans should govern Ireland without the control of the English Parliament. English colonists in America believed similarly that they should govern there, independent of English control.

The American Revolution:

In 1776, the American colonists rose in rebellion against Britain over trade restrictions. This became a full-scale war. Many Irish settlers who had emigrated to America joined the rebel force.

Britain sent troops to America, to quell the rebellion, and some of these were diverted from duty in Ireland. In the absence of these troops, Protestant citizens in Ireland organized themselves into their own special army, which was called the Volunteers. They sympathised with the American cause, and asked Britain to grant them some independence. They became a political force and under the leadership of Henry Grattan the movement grew and forced the British government to relax some of the Laws of Trade. Poyning's Law of 1494 was removed, and some Catholic rights were re-established. Briefly it seemed that Ireland would regain a great deal of independence, but in 1789 a new threat emerged in European politics.

The French Revolution:

Inspired by the success of the American rebel forces, who had won their war of independence, the middle classes of France led a revolution against the monarch, the nobility and the Church. Social and economic distress convinced the ordinary people that they should support the revolution.

Years of social injustice had been one of the major causes of the French Revolution. This cartoon shows a French peasant carrying a bishop and a nobleman on his back. The wealthy in France did not pay taxes, and the peasants did. The situation in Ireland was similar.

Political ideas:

Two books were particularly important in shaping people's thoughts. A British writer, Tom Paine, published a book called *The Rights of Man* in 1791 and 1792. Jean-Jacques Rousseau, a French writer, published a book called *Du Contrat Social* (*The Social Contract*). One of the most important phrases of the time came from Rousseau's book: *l'homme est né libre, et partout il est dans les fers* – "Man is born free, and everywhere is in chains". But Paine's work was even more radical in opinion. It attacked the monarchy, rich people and the Church, and said that this system of government should be destroyed.

Paine's ideas spread to Ireland, France and mainland Europe, and America. His book was widely read and deeply discussed. It was a best seller in England, and when Part One was published in 1791 it sold 50,000 copies at a cost of 3 shillings a book. Part Two was equally successful. It is estimated that 200,000 copies were sold by 1809. Paine's ideas were not original, but they caught the attention of the reading public at a fortunate time. The book was banned by the British government because of its revolutionary ideas.

IRISH REVOLU- TIONARIES

The Volunteers were of Protestant background and asked for constitutional reform. The United Irishmen, founded in 1791 and led by Wolfe Tone, appealed to Protestants and Catholics to join together and form an Irish revolutionary party, based on French ideas. Two political, working-class clubs were started in Belfast and Dublin in the autumn of 1791, and the United Irishmen excluded any discussion which might arouse sectarian differences. Their demands were similar to those of British radicals who wished for reform of the political system.

The connection with France, and with the French Revolution, caused the British government to view the United Irishmen as "Fifth Columnists" in Ireland, and as traitors. Anyone who supported French ideas was assumed to be a spy for France and could be hanged for treason. New laws were passed in 1793 which suppressed political freedom, and the clubs were closed in May 1794. Wolfe Tone was expelled from Ireland and went to France. He returned in 1796, at the head of an invasion force, hoping to establish a republic both in Ireland and in England. His plans were not to succeed, as his ships were battered by gale force winds. This was a particularly dangerous moment, and confirmed previously stated beliefs that Ireland should be British-controlled territory. Tone tried again in 1797 and the expedition failed. France would not help any more, and so the Irish people rose in support of Tone by themselves in 1798.

BECOMING A REVOLUTIONARY

The oath of the United Irishmen:

This is part of the political examination given to United Irishmen who supported the idea of revolution. The clubs were banned, and the swearing in of new members was carefully controlled. Everything was done with secrecy because government spies might have infiltrated the group. The candidate was examined first, and then swore an oath of secrecy. The green bough which is mentioned refers to the idea of liberty being a tree which could be planted in a country. The colour chosen by the radicals was green.

Ques. What have you got in your hand?
Ans. A green bough.
Ques. Where did it first grow?
Ans. In America.
Ques. Where did it bud?
Ans. In France.
Ques. Where are you going to plant it?
Ans. In the Crown of Great Britain.

Another group of revolutionaries were the Catholic Defenders. They were more concerned with economic changes, and hoped to get changes in tithes, rents and taxation. They sometimes organized meetings in their chapels, and they also took oaths of secrecy. Many revolutionaries were involved in organizing local reading sessions of political books, newspapers and handbills, so that those who were unable to read were kept informed of current events.

COERCION

A travelling gallows, which was used by the British troops in Ireland, to suppress rebellion in 1798. Pitch-capping was also used as a means of torture. Pitch mixed with gunpowder was pressed over the skull and then set alight.

From 1794 to 1796 was a time of great unrest in Ireland. The British government decided on a policy of coercion, or force. They sent in extra troops, increasing the number of British soldiers serving in Ireland to 140,000 over this period. Drafting in extra troops became the normal method of dealing with unrest in Ireland from this time onwards. Further plots were discovered in 1797 and 1798, and the army applied savage and systematic flogging of Irish people to obtain evidence of guilt. Throughout Ireland people were tortured, arrested and shot. Landowners in Ireland saw the policy of coercion, and recognized the dangers it might bring. Thoughts of the French revolution made them fear for their lives.

The savage treatment of the people did not stop a planned uprising in 1798. This was easily crushed except in Wexford, where Catholics turned on Protestants and massacred many families. Wolfe Tone landed in Ireland, but was defeated, captured and committed suicide. Another member of the United Irishmen, Napper Tandy, escaped capture, and was remembered in the song, "The Wearing of the Green".

Feelings ran high in these years, and colours were important in distinguishing different political viewpoints.

A green bonnet:

In May, 1798, the narrator . . . donned her bonnet of the previous season [which] was of bright green silk . . . Amid other signs of the times, "the wearing of the green" came to be regarded with suspicion and dislike by the authorities of the day. Of this, however, the wearer of the green bonnet was then quite unconscious . . . she was startled to hear, every other moment, a voice whispering, almost under her bonnet: "God bless your colour, ma'am!" She remarked that those who did not use this phrase regarded her with an angry scowl. . .

(*Source:* an interview of Mrs Anastasia O'Byrne, recorded in 1889, when she was over 100 years old. It was written down by W.J. Fitzpatrick. Quoted in J. Carty (ed.) *Ireland 1783-1850*, C.J. Fallon, 1949)

In Ulster, Protestants clashed with Catholics, and there were violent scenes between rival groups. There were rival secret societies, which had formed because of the need for agricultural reform. The Protestant "Peep O'Day Boys" and the Catholic Defenders shared similar problems, but could not agree on co-existence, because of sectarian differences. The societies were infiltrated by government spies, and information extracted led to further arrests, floggings and hangings.

A green string:

Here I found soldiers going about the country burning the houses of suspected United Irishmen. Near to Armagh I met a group of Orangemen decorated with cockades. They were obliging everyone to take off every article of green they wore. I had a green string to my umbrella, and so, in fear lest I be mistaken for a rebel, I cut it off.

(*Source:* Le Chevalier de la Tocnaye, *A Frenchman's Walk Through Ireland, 1796-1797*)

Can we believe the account of Mrs Anastasia O'Byrne when she says that she was not aware of the meaning of the radical "bright green"?

What evidence does Le Chevalier de la Tocnaye give of the behaviour of British troops in Ireland?

IRELAND AND ENGLAND UNITED

The Protestants formed a special society in 1795. It was called the Loyal Orange Association, and took its name from William of Orange. It vowed loyalty to the Crown of England, if the monarch remained loyal to the Protestant Ascendancy, and began to celebrate every year the Battle of the Boyne. The organization was based on sectarian differences, and grew swiftly in Ulster.

When the rebellion of 1798 had been crushed, the British Prime Minister, Pitt, put forward plans for uniting Ireland and England. Many Catholics and Protestants in Ireland refused to accept Pitt's proposals. To get his bill passed, Pitt bribed members of the Irish Parliament, and in 1800 the Act of Union was passed by the Irish House of Commons. Ireland lost an independent Parliament, as power was transferred to Westminster. Any change to be effected would have to be centred on British politics, and discussed in London.

ON REFLECTION:

Both Orange supporters and Irish "revolutionaries" faced the same problems of agrarian hardship. What had led to the division between the opposing groups?

Would you say that the evidence shows that the discontent in the eighteenth century relates to social and economic distress, rather than to the cause of nationalism?

The Act of Union did not affect poor people in Ireland. Their lives continued to be full of hardship and poverty. If they wanted social and economic change how would they obtain it from the Westminster Parliament?

By 1800 many of the Penal Laws had fallen into disuse. Catholics had been given the vote in 1780, but only the rich were allowed to use it, and Catholics could still not take office. How would this affect Catholic representation in politics?

The Great Starvation

There are some episodes in the history of Ireland which have lived on in the memory of groups of people, continuing to affect the ways they feel and think. Two such episodes for Protestants are the Siege of Derry and the Battle of the Boyne. The potato blight, which caused widescale famine from 1845 to 1849, left a legacy of bitterness and hatred in Catholic minds. As a result of the famine, the political events of the nineteenth and twentieth centuries were focused on the issues of land and independence from British rule.

AGRICULTURAL PRACTICES

Agricultural labourers in Ireland survived on the production of potatoes. This root crop had been introduced into Europe in the seventeenth century, and had flourished in Ireland. There were many benefits for the people. Potatoes were easy to grow, they put minerals into the soil, and, because they grew underground, they were less easy to destroy in times of civil unrest. Potatoes could support a much larger number of people per acre than other crops. They prevented scurvy, which was endemic among the European poor, and could be used as animal fodder. Relying on only one crop had its dangers. If the potato crop failed, there was no alternative food for the Irish people. This is what occurred between 1845 and 1849.

Visitors to Ireland had always remarked on two aspects of agricultural life. One was the actual fertility of the land, which was capable of maintaining a high level of production. The other was the poverty of Irish agricultural labourers, and the miserable conditions in which they lived. Such conditions were not unusual in Europe at this time, but in Ireland between 1800 and 1845 there had been a vast population explosion which had doubled the number of people to be fed. Population figures rose from approximately four and a half million to eight million over a period of forty years. The 1841 census gave the population of Ireland as 8,175,124.

The plots of land on which people survived were small, and any cereal crops which were grown were sold to pay the enormously high rents demanded by landlords. Secret societies called Land Leagues had been formed to fight "rack-renting" and eviction. They organized the people in a locality to resist high rents and subsequent eviction for non-payment.

In some areas the Land Leagues had strong leaders and real power. They could prevent others from taking land left vacant after an eviction and so the landlord was unable to collect rent and was forced to reconsider his decision. In the later part of the nineteenth century the Land Leagues grew much stronger, until there was open "war" between landowner and tenants over rents and security of tenure. However, on a national level, the Leagues were not a successful movement, as they lacked political organization.

The British government, which had the means to stop the distress, chose laissez-faire policies instead. This meant that it would not interfere with the natural progress of society. Both politicians and landlords in Ireland accepted poverty as a necessary evil, and the threat of famine as part of "nature's remedy" for an over-populated country.

Other areas of the British Empire relied on monoculture for economic survival. Compare the system of slavery and sugar production in the West Indies to the conditions of life for Irish agricultural labourers in the eighteenth and nineteenth centuries.

The Land Leagues relied on intimidation and sometimes violence to achieve their goals. Did they have alternatives?

THE YEARS OF FAMINE BEGIN

The spores carrying the potato blight came from mainland Britain and Europe. They were carried by wind, rain and insects. The evidence which follows outlines the story of the years of famine.

The people grow hungry:

Cowering wretches almost naked in the savage weather, prowling in turnip fields and endeavouring to grub up roots that had been left. . . . And sometimes I could see in front of the cottages little children leaning against a fence – for they could not stand – their limbs fleshless, their bodies half naked, their faces bloated yet wrinkled and of a pale greenish hue – children who could never, oh it was too plain, grow up to be men and women.

(*Source:* John Mitchell, *The last conquest of Ireland (perhaps)*, published in 1861)

Winter, 1846-47:

A modern historian described the onset of these winter months:

Autumn was now passing into winter. The nettles and blackberries, the edible roots and cabbage leaves on which hundreds of people had been eking out an existence disappeared; flocks of wretched beings, resembling human scarecrows, had combed the blighted potato fields over and over again until not a fragment of a potato that was conceivably edible remained. . .
At this moment of suffering unprecedented weather added greatly to the misery of the people. The climate of Ireland is famous for its mildness; years pass without a fall of snow; in the gardens of the south and west semi-tropical plants flourish. . . . In 1846, at the end of October it became cold, and in November snow began to fall.

(*Source:* Cecil Woodham Smith, *The Great Hunger*, Hamish Hamilton Ltd, 1962)

Many Irish people had sold their possessions for food, and had little warm clothing to protect themselves against the cold. The British government had begun to organize public work schemes, but many people were too ill and cold to work at all. With no money to buy food, thousands starved to death in the winter of 1846 and through the early months of 1847.

AID FOR THE FAMINE VICTIMS

Famine charity appeals:

When English people eventually learned of the horrors of the famine in Ireland, charity organizations began to collect money. £14,000 was sent from India, and was the first sum of money to be raised. This was collected from many of the Irish troops, who served in the army in India. The Irish Relief Association, Ladies' Work Associations, and the central Relief Committee of the Society of Friends (the Quakers) all began to organize campaigns.

Government assistance:

Ireland was within twelve hours' reach of one of the wealthiest countries in the world. Between 1845 and 1849 an estimated one million of its people died of famine and disease. The British Prime Minister, Sir Robert Peel, led the Conservative Party. He made arrangements to import cheap American maize for distribution in Ireland, but insisted that wherever possible the Irish people should pay for it. The government also continued to allow the export of Irish arable farm produce as usual.

There were problems attached to the import of the American maize. It was not fit for export until several months after harvesting, and all the European countries competed for a share of the produce. There was not enough to feed the Irish people through the long winter months, and the price of the maize was too high for most families. The store-houses, which were guarded by the police, were opened in the west of Ireland, and those affected by the famine elsewhere were not provided with government supplies.

American maize was low in vitamins and unsuited to the needs of famine victims. There were few facilities for grinding the maize, and the government recommended boiling the corn for an hour and a half before eating it. This did little to soften the corn, and eating it this way caused severe stomach pains. Despite this, the depots were always surrounded by people, and food riots occurred.

1847: PLAGUE YEAR

The poor move to the towns and workhouses:

Under the Irish Poor Law Act of 1838, Ireland had 130 Poor Law Unions, which were responsible for building local workhouses. They were to be run by collecting a rate for the poor, but few had been able to open, and when the famine struck, they were closed, often in disrepair and in debt. By 1847 the workhouse system was bankrupt, but thousands of people were arriving seeking relief.

As the people moved to the towns and workhouses, disease travelled with them: 1847 became known as the Plague Year. Cholera, smallpox, dysentery, typhus fever and relapsing fever attacked the migrant population, and the death rate soared. Tents were erected in towns to cater for those who had disease, and this eased the burden on the workhouses. By November 1847, the epidemics were beginning to slow down, but there were still outbreaks of fever throughout the following year. In December 1848, Asiatic Cholera entered Belfast and added to the death toll.

The migration from the country begins. This picture shows the Irish poor crowding round the gates of a workhouse for food and shelter.

The Soup Kitchen Act:

In 1847 the government passed a Soup Kitchen Act which gave charities and local committees some small financial aid. Thereafter the government declared that it was up to the people of Ireland to provide help for themselves.

A fashionable London chef, Alexis Soyer, "created" a soup for the poor of London. It cost three farthings a quart, and was thought to be "very good and nourishing". He had no understanding of the full effects of famine. The government was warned that soup was actually harmful for people suffering from starvation, as it passed straight through the body giving no nourishment. For people suffering from dysentery it could cause death.

Quarter lb of leg of beef – 1d.
2 gallons of water
2 ozs of dripping – ½d.
2 onions and other vegetables – 2d.
½ lb flour – a farthing
½ lb pearl barley – 1½d.
3 ozs salt and ½ oz brown sugar

(*Source:* quoted in Cecil Woodham Smith, *The Great Hunger*, Hamish Hamilton, 1962)

Alexis Soyer was invited to Ireland, where he opened a Model Soup Kitchen in Dublin. The people flooded into Dublin when they heard of the distribution of food. The soup left them as hungry as before. The government turned Soyer's kitchen over to the Relief Committee of the South Dublin Union. Other soup kitchens were opened across Ireland, and hungry, desperate people fought each other to receive a share. The relief committees and workhouses could not take care of the needy. Thousands more starved to death in the winter of 1847-48.

THE WEST OF IRELAND

Those in the west of Ireland suffered the greatest hardship. Seed was too expensive to buy, and in short supply. Farming was neglected because the people had to find employment through the public work schemes. It was impossible to live off fishing because the local fishing boat, the curragh, was not suitable for deep-sea fishing, and the gales on the west coast were too strong. All pawnable possessions were sold for food, and these included boats and rigging. Edible seaweed, turnips, cabbage leaves and weeds fed the people of County Mayo.

LANDLORDS AND TENANTS

Landlords varied in attitude towards their tenants. Some refused to collect rents from those they knew were destitute, and subsidized their tenants, as far as they could. Others were more unscrupulous, and used non-payment of rent as an excuse to clear their estates of tenants. Some offered payment for the passage to Britain, or to America and Canada, on condition that the tenants' houses were "tumbled" – that is, pulled apart so that no more tenants could move in.

EMIGRATION

From 1847, ever-increasing numbers of Irish people decided to emigrate. One and a half million people left Ireland during the famine years. In 1847 the mass emigrations were of the very poor Irish peasants, but in 1848 richer farmers began to leave, too.

1848-49

During 1848 Ireland was once again in rebellion, as was the rest of Europe. All over the continent governments fell, and were replaced by representatives of the people. In Ireland a small group of radicals led a revolt against the British government, but this was unsuccessful and provoked much anger. The British government had been reluctant before to offer help for Ireland's poor: now, attitudes hardened, and reprisals were stern. Troops were drafted in again to maintain order. The Young Irelanders were imprisoned and transported. Then, in 1849, after one year of healthy farming, the potato crop failed again.

The population continued to drop, as more families chose to emigrate. It is estimated that approximately two and a half million Irish people died of starvation or disease, or emigrated, from 1845 to 1849. The 1851 census recorded 6,552,385 people, but this can only be an estimate, as it was impossible to record deaths accurately during the years of famine. Failure of crops continued to be a problem throughout the rest of the nineteenth century.

The movement of population brought about social and economic changes in the way people lived in Ireland. It also created strongly anti-British attitudes in those who settled abroad, in Canada and America, and this was to have an important effect upon politics in the twentieth century.

ON REFLECTION:

Consider the descriptions of Ireland written by Spenser in the sixteenth century (page 17) in relation to the years of famine in the nineteenth century. What were the main factors which accounted for the deaths in both the sixteenth and the nineteenth centuries?

Oral history plays an important part in the education of young people. What attitudes might have been transferred to children by those who had lived through the events of the Irish famine?

Many Irish people refer to this period as The Great Starvation. In most textbooks it is referred to as the Irish Famine. Can you explain why there is this difference in terminology?

Many people who spoke Gaelic died at this time. What is important about the use of language in a nationalistic sense? Why has this modern Irish poet chosen to write in Gaelic? What does the memory of the famine mean to him?

1845

Lá a raibh
each dubh gan mharcach
ar chosa in airde
ag tóirniú
ar chrúba
ciúine

Lá a raibh
fallaing ag leathadh
a dorchacht
thar learga na gcnoc
lá a dtáinig
spealadóirí
gan súile

Lá dá bhfaca
naomhóga anaithnid
gan duladh ar an bpoll
céaslaí i lámha
marbhán

Lá a ndeachaigh
spealadóir
gan súil ina cheann
ar mhuin eich dhuibh
gur ghluais currracháin
go tamhanda roighin
i dtres mo thíre

1845

The day
a riderless horse
thundered
at full gallop
on hooves
of silence

The day
a cloak spread
its darkness
across the mountain
when the eyeless
reapers
came

The day
strange boats were seen
unmoving on the bay
oars gripped by hands
of deadmen

The day
a reaper
with empty eye sockets
mounted
the black steed
the boats
swung their prows
towards our shores

Thomás Mac Síomóin

(*Source: Ireland and the Arts*, ed. Tim Pat Coogan (Literary Review), published by Namara Press)

Industrialization and Imperialism

The American and French Revolutions had an enormous effect on how people responded to ideas in political thought. In some cases this brought about radical, lasting change. In social and economic terms, too, Europe was witnessing revolution.

IRISH INDUSTRY Textile production was organized on an informal, domestic basis in the eighteenth century. A family would be involved in the whole process of producing fabric, from carding and spinning to weaving and dyeing. The money they earned from this was added to their income from farming. Both England and Ireland produced woollen cloth, but Ireland's industry was prohibited in 1699 because it competed with England's textile production.

Irish weavers developed linen as an alternative to wool. The flax they used for making the linen was either imported or grown on small plots of land, and the process of linen production provided a part-time job for farmers. Irish weavers were not allowed to export coloured linens to Britain, but the industry grew successful because they could export to the British colonies of North America and the West Indies.

The linen industry was most heavily concentrated in Ulster, and Belfast began to replace Dublin as the commercial centre of Ireland. Ulster had always had a distinctly separate character, and the people benefited from a greater security of tenure than those living elsewhere. During the years of famine the people of Ulster felt the pressures of hardship less than those who were living in the south and west of Ireland.

Dublin was the second largest city in the United Kingdom in the early eighteenth century, but within a hundred years it had been overtaken by Belfast. Belfast's prosperity was built on a new system of work, and on cotton and steel production. Over the nineteenth century the population of Dublin increased to 300,000, while in Belfast the population increased from 100,000 to 400,000.

BELFAST AND THE NORTH OF IRELAND'S PLACE WITHIN THE BRITISH EMPIRE The revolution that had occurred in Belfast was the introduction of the factory system. During the eighteenth century products, such as cotton, of the British colonies in the West Indies would come in to British ports and from there the raw goods were either re-exported or transferred to the "finishing" industries. The domestic system of industry was replaced by new methods of production as new machinery and an organized system of labour were brought in.

As Britain became the leading industrial nation, the territories ruled by the Westminster Parliament produced goods for Britain. After the Act of Union, Belfast became the leading industrial city of Ireland, and served the needs of the second British Empire which developed during the Victorian era.

Raw cotton was imported from the West Indies, India and America. For a brief period the American Civil War caused a "cotton famine" in Ireland

and the linen industry expanded. Manufacturing profits rose from £6¼ million to £10 million by 1864. After 1865, growth in both linen and cotton exports from Ireland gradually declined. The industry continued to run on female labour and wages remained low.

The engineering skills which had been needed to produce textile machinery were now applied in a different way. Edward Harland founded a shipbuilding yard which turned Belfast into a national and international engineering and shipbuilding centre. The experiments in iron ships produced the famous *Titanic*. Belfast experienced a massive increase in migrants during this period. Catholics settled in the Falls Road area of Belfast, and Protestants in the Shankhill Road. Where the two communities came into contact, there were often disturbances.

By the middle of the nineteenth century Belfast was the most prosperous city in Ireland, and one of the largest cities in Great Britain. Roads and ports were developed to provide the necessary transport links. *Laissez-faire* policies were in operation in Ireland, and large industries were allowed to develop. The rest of Ireland suffered, as it lacked large-scale industry or concentrated on agriculture. Although the working classes in both Britain and Ireland had a higher standard of living as a result of industrialization, the Irish economy still lagged behind.

The British Empire was at its height over this period, and Belfast industry benefited from this. Irish industrialists valued the British connection, and wished to retain it. Belfast could not survive without the support of British industry, which supplied the raw resources it lacked of iron, steel and coal. Its shipbuilding industry was the backbone of the British navy, and the strength of the navy controlled the sea lanes to the British Empire.

RACISM Because Britain was so powerful, it was possible for British people to believe that they were racially superior to those who lived in the lands conquered by British armies, and linked by the British navy. The Irish people were amongst those viewed as an inferior race. The Irish playwright J.M. Synge wrote about the effects of anti-Irish attitudes. As a young writer he became deeply involved in the Gaelic revival movement, which aimed to restore the place of Irish history which had been rejected by English writers and historians. He considered that the anti-Irish bias in English writing could only be described as racist.

It should never be forgotten that half the troubles of England and Ireland have arisen from . . . ignorance based on the biased view of . . . historians and on the absurd caricatures which . . . have achieved much in the way of making the Irish character a sealed book to the Englishman.

(*Source:* quoted in *Nothing But The Same Old Story. The Roots of Anti-Irish Racism,* Information on Ireland, 1984)

Scientific racism had some intellectual followers in the nineteenth century. The people who studied this believed in white supremacy. The people who lived in Germany, Britain and America were the most civilized and successful. Other Europeans came next. Indians, Africans, Chinese and Aborigines were all considered inferior because of their racial origin.

Some scientists believed that people could be grouped according to the size and shape of their skulls. These drawings show how they tried to explain their ideas. Negros and Irish people were considered primitive because they had lived isolated lives. English and German people were superior because they had competed successfully against other nations in the world. They were part of a white master race.

IRISH IBERIAN.　　ANGLO-TEUTONIC.　　NEGRO.

Compare the following extract with the illustration. How could these ideas be used to justify British rule of Ireland?

This extract comes from a letter written by Charles Kingsley to his wife in 1860. He had been to Ireland on holiday.

I am haunted by the human chimpanzees I saw along that hundred miles of horrible country . . . to see white chimpanzees is dreadful; if they were black, one would not see it so much, but their skins, except where tanned by exposure, are as white as ours.

Kingsley was a famous nineteenth-century novelist. He also had close connections with a small socialist group called the Fabians. Some of these were supporters of the British Empire and strongly racist in their views about the peoples who were governed by the British Parliament.

Can you tell, from looking at the illustration, why Kingsley regards the Irish as "human chimpanzees"?

If you saw this kind of picture and read such views in a science book, would your ideas be influenced?

Does this type of propaganda explain why Synge felt so strongly about "biased historians" and British racism?

In mid-Victorian Britain there was a sense of security in the knowledge that Britain was the most powerful country in the world. This power came from winning wars and annexing land. Why were white Europeans so successful in their building of empires outside Europe?

Attitudes like this were quite common in nineteenth-century Britain and Europe. Friedrich Engels, a close friend of Karl Marx, the founder of the idea of Communism, wrote a book called *The Condition of the Working Classes in England.* Many of the large industrial towns had growing communities of Irish migrants, who lived in appalling poverty. Engels describes their houses, and animals, and condemns them as lazy and filthy. Similar attitudes were expressed by Canadians and Americans who lived in areas where there were large groups of Irish migrants.

IRISH AND INDIAN NATIONALISTS

Some Irish nationalists saw a need to unite with others within the British Empire, so that the fight for political freedom would have more strength. The links between Ireland and India were clear to Irish nationalists. Both countries were ruled by the British Parliament, and had a standing army to maintain law and order. Many soldiers of the British army in India were Irish. The army in which they served kept order in India and in Ireland. Amongst Irish soldiers in the Indian army, and Irish nationalists in Ireland, there was sympathy for the Indians who were ruled by Britain.

An Irish nationalist speaks out against the British Empire:

If the people of Ireland have a right to their own country, the people of India have as just a claim to theirs; if it is wrong to plunder the Irish, it is also wrong to plunder the Hindoos; but if, on the other hand, it is justifiable in Irishmen to go forth to rob and enslave the Hindoos, and Ashantees, and other peoples, then we say, it is justifiable in Danes and Normans and Saxons to rob and enslave the Irish.

(*Source:* written by Patrick Ford, a Fenian, in an American newspaper, the *New York Irish World*, 12 August 1876. The paper was smuggled into Ireland each week.)

There were some Indian nationalists who expressed similar feelings of sympathy for Irish people, and could see that there were wider implications than just fighting for freedom in India or Ireland. However, such attitudes were rare. The Indian and Irish nationalist movements were to develop separately. Irish politics were to be dominated by the constitutional attitudes of two important Irish politicians who focused attention solely on the Anglo-Irish connection.

ON REFLECTION:

The divisions between rich and poor led to political revolution in eighteenth-century Ireland. What divisions were created by social and economic developments in the nineteenth century?

Think about the changes which occurred between the creation of the first British Empire and the emergence of the second British Empire of the mid-nineteenth century. How had Britain's imperial policy reshaped Ireland's history?

Britain had acquired a huge empire by the mid-nineteenth century. It stretched from Canada to New Zealand, and included India, Australia and large parts of Africa. The Royal Navy controlled the sea routes and kept contact between the peoples of the British Empire. What special place did Belfast hold in the imperial policy of Great Britain?

A Constitutional Dilemma

BRITAIN, IRELAND AND NINETEENTH-CENTURY POLITICS

In 1801 the Act of Union came into force, and Westminster became the centre for political debate. There were many demands for reform within Britain in the nineteenth century. "The Irish Question" was only one of many issues hotly debated by the British Parliament. As the century progressed, Ireland came to the forefront of British political life, and dominated "party" politics.

DANIEL O'CONNELL AND THE CATHOLIC ASSOCIATION

Daniel O'Connell became the leader of a new political organization called the Catholic Association, in 1823. He was the first Catholic to stand for election in Ireland for 150 years. The Association demanded full Catholic emancipation, since discrimination still existed within the Irish political system. Ordinary people felt that they could give support to the Association because it represented their viewpoint, and this made it the first major mass movement in the political history of Britain.

In 1828 they elected Daniel O'Connell to Parliament, but this was against the law. Fearing another Irish rebellion, the British government passed the Catholic Emancipation Act in 1829, and Daniel O'Connell took up his seat at the Westminster Parliament as an elected Member of Parliament for Clare. From 1841 he began to lead a movement for the repeal of the Act of Union. He organized a series of "monster meetings" which drew enormous crowds. From this description of Daniel O'Connell, which was written by an Irish radical, see if you can understand why O'Connell was so popular with the Irish people.

[He was] . . . a man of gigantic proportions in body and in mind; with no profound learning . . . but with a vast and varied knowledge of human nature . . . with a voice like thunder and earthquake, yet musical and soft at will . . . he had the power to make other men hate or love, laugh or weep at his good pleasure.

(*Source:* Introduction to The Jail Journal written by John Mitchell, 1848, quoted in *Ireland 1783-1850*, James Carty (ed.), C.J. Fallon Ltd, 1949)

One "monster meeting" was held at Tara. Why did O'Connell pick that site?

The open-air meetings gathered thousands of people together. As they considered such large crowds dangerous, the British government sent in reinforcements of soldiers to control them. However, there was little need for the troops, as the meetings were conducted without the use of violence. O'Connell hated the use of force, and believed strongly in employing constitutional means to gain political change. At the Tara meeting the crowd exceeded 500,000 people.

Daniel O'Connell could not gather enough support in the Westminster Parliament for repealing the Act of Union. He spent time in prison for his

KING O'CONNELL AT TARA.

How does this Punch *cartoon portray an alternative view of O'Connell? How do you account for the different view it expresses? In what way has the cartoonist portrayed the people who are kneeling around O'Connell?*

political activities, witnessed the outbreak of famine in 1846, and died in 1847, having lost support to younger radicals who had formed the Young Ireland party. They founded a newspaper, *The Nation*, and used it to express their ideas. The most famous contributors included Thomas Davis, Charles Gavan Duffy, James Fintan Lalor and John Mitchell. The ideas for which they argued ranged from the reform of the land system by introducing fair rents and security of tenure, to nationalism and home rule for Ireland.

REPUBLICANS

Daniel O'Connell led a nationalist movement which he believed should continue Ireland's political connection with Great Britain. However, others saw Ireland's future differently. Supporters of republicanism in the French revolutionary tradition rejected any future connection with Britain, the monarchy and the Empire. They did not reject the idea of using force to achieve their independence. There were some small risings against Britain, none of which were successful. In 1803 Robert Emmet led a republican uprising, and was tried and executed. In 1848, the Young Irelanders led a rising in sympathy with revolutions in Europe, but they were easily crushed by the British government. On 17 March 1858, James Stephens founded a secret society which was to become known as the Irish Republican Brotherhood, or Fenians. The uprising it planned in 1867 was also a failure, despite financial support from Irish settlers in America and Canada.

THE LAND WAR AND THE BRITISH GOVERNMENT'S RESPONSE

After O'Connell's death the Irish Parliamentary Party continued to exist and grew again under the leadership of Isaac Butt. In 1872 he founded the Irish Home Rule Party. However, politics at Westminster seemed far removed from the Land War which was being waged in Ireland between landlords and tenants. This was organized by Michael Davitt, who founded the Irish Land League in 1879, and was supported by agrarian societies and the Fenians. After the famine years, and because of the bitterness felt towards Britain, there was strong support also from ordinary people in Ireland. The

Land War gave the Irish Parliamentary Party a political issue to take to Westminster.

In 1868 William Gladstone became the Liberal Prime Minister of Britain. He was convinced that it was important to solve the problem of the government of Ireland. His first ministry was responsible for disestablishing the Anglican Church in Ireland, removing church tithes which had to be paid by the people, and for a Land Act which allowed compensation for eviction. Compensation was also given to people who had improved their land, and had been unable to claim a reduction in rent because of their hard work. Gladstone's act was essentially "English" in attitude, and did nothing to satisfy Irish demands for the "three Fs" — Fair rent, Fixity of tenure and Freedom of sale.

The British government tried to deal with the Land War by coercion, and more troops were drafted into Ireland. Many of the leaders of the Land League were arrested and imprisoned. Between 1881 and 1900 new acts were passed which made land tenure in Ireland fairer, and put the balance back in favour of Irish tenant farmers. In 1881 Land Courts were established which had power to fix rents fairly. By 1900 the British government was buying out landlords, offering mortgages to tenants and giving them the right to own the land on which they had lived and worked. These new laws had come too late, however, to prevent the growth of a militant Home Rule Party which demanded freedom from British rule. This new party represented over half of the total Irish seats in the Westminster Parliament. It focused on the issues of land and independence.

THE HOME RULE PARTY AND CHARLES STEWART PARNELL

Charles Stewart Parnell, a Protestant landowner in Ireland, gained the leadership of the Irish Home Rule Party in 1879. He led the Irish MPs in the Westminster Parliament and his party held the balance of power between the Liberals and Conservatives. He moved Irish politics to the forefront of the British political scene by adopting obstruction techniques in Parliament to slow down the process of law-making and debate. This is known as filibustering. The Home Rule Party wanted Ireland to control all decisions on domestic affairs. Foreign policy would still be directed by Britain.

In the Land War, the number of evictions rose and reprisals were the response. Parnell agreed to support Gladstone's 1881 Land Act. Irish priests fought side by side with Irish people. The *leaders* of the Catholic Church in Ireland sided with British leaders, and opposed the nationalist movement. The Land League and the Catholic masses gave support to Parnell.

Revolutionary groups abroad, in America and Canada, collected money for the Irish cause. They used unconventional methods to achieve their goal. The first bombs in London were exploded and Clerkenwell Jail was blown up in 1867. The IRB, or Fenians, as they were known, after the legendary third-century AD army which had served the High King of Tara, were divided between those for and those against Parnell's Parliamentary methods. On the whole they supported him.

The Irish Home Rule Party suffered a temporary setback in 1882 when the Chief Secretary for Ireland was assassinated. It recovered, and Parnell continued to develop an authoritative role in Parliament. He was at the height of his power from 1880 to 1888.

The election results, November 1885:

```
Liberals ......................... 335
Conservatives ............... 249
The Home Rule Party ....... 86
```

Parnell's party supported the Conservatives in this election.

In April 1886 Gladstone introduced his Home Rule Bill. By this time Parnell's party supported the Liberals. The Protestants in Ulster showed their dislike of the bill by drilling and demonstration. Joseph Chamberlain split the Liberal vote by forming a new group called the Liberal Unionists, which supported the Ulster Protestants. He was strongly committed to the British Empire, and to a policy of imperialism.

Why would an imperialist like Chamberlain think the prospect of Home Rule for Ireland dangerous?

What other motives might a politician have for leading an opposition group from within his or her political party?

Chamberlain declared that he would "Kill the Bill". Lord Randolph Churchill, a member of the Conservative Party, decided that the Protestant cause against Irish Home Rule would be a sound political issue for the opposition party to take up. He decided to "play the Orange Card". Protestants of all classes and the Conservative Party joined forces against the threat of Home Rule. The Liberal Unionists refused to vote for Gladstone's Home Rule Bill, and the defeat of the government forced an election in 1886. The House of Lords used its veto, and voted out Home Rule.

The election results, 1886:

```
Liberals ......................... 191
Conservatives ............... 316
Liberal Unionists ............. 78
Irish Home Rule Party ...... 85
Total ............................ 670
```

How much support had Gladstone's Liberal Party lost because of the revolt of the Liberal Unionists?

What effect could the Liberal Unionists have on the balance of power at Westminster?

By how much has the Conservative Party increased its support?

Compare these results to those of 1885. How had Parnell's party suffered by these political changes?

ULSTER WILL FIGHT AND ULSTER WILL BE RIGHT On a local level, in Ireland, the Protestant Orange movement was organized in lodges. The original society was sectarian and working-class. It grew in strength by recruiting the textile and shipping workers in Belfast, and now it began to gather support from the upper classes as well. Lord Randolph

Churchill's visit to Belfast in 1886 encouraged the Unionists and Orange lodges to display their strength. The slogan of the time was fashioned by Churchill: "Ulster will fight, and Ulster will be right". On his return to England later that year, Churchill pledged support for their cause. This move was warmly welcomed by members of the new Conservative government. The Orange cause was to be openly supported by British Conservatives throughout the early years of the twentieth century. Individual Orange lodges continued to recruit new members, and held drilling sessions in Belfast. This created an unsettling and provocative atmosphere, and an increase in sectarian disturbances followed. The Orange Order maintained its right to be linked to Britain, in a Protestant Ulster.

PARNELL LOSES POLITICAL POWER

Charles Stewart Parnell. He lost political power because of a personal domestic issue. Do you think a politician should be forced to choose between a career and personal relationships?

In 1882 Parnell was accused of being involved in the murder of the Chief Secretary of Ireland. The Irish Home Rule Party had close connections with the Irish Republican Brotherhood and the Land League, both of which played a part in the murder. Parnell's party suffered a major setback in public image because of this. In 1889 he was cited in a divorce case.

Parnell had been involved in a long-term relationship with Kitty O'Shea, who was married to an Irishman. The evidence given in court was embarrassing, and impossible to deny. When the scandal became public knowledge through the newspapers, the Irish Home Rule Party and the British political parties became deeply divided between those who supported Parnell and those who did not. The Catholic Church condemned Parnell.

In 1890 the Home Rule Party voted on Parnell's position as leader of the Party, and the vote was against him by 45 to 29.

James Joyce grew up in Dublin and was educated as a Catholic. In this extract from his autobiography, he remembers as a little boy, hearing the adults around him argue over the fall of Parnell:

– And can we not love our country then? asked Mr Casey. Are we not to follow the man that was born to lead us?
– A traitor to his country! replied Dante. A traitor, an adulterer! The priests were right to abandon him. The priests were always the true friends of Ireland. . . . God and religion before everything! Dante cried. God and religion before the world!
Mr. Casey raised his clenched fist and brought it down on the table with a crash.
– Very well, then he shouted hoarsely, if it comes to that, no God for Ireland! . . . We have had too much God in Ireland. Away with God!
– Blasphemer! Devil! screamed Dante, starting to her feet and almost spitting in his face. . . .
Devil out of hell! We won! We crushed him to death! Fiend!
The door slammed behind her.
Mr. Casey . . . suddenly bowed his hands in his head with a sob of pain.
– Poor Parnell! he cried loudly. My dead king!
He sobbed bitterly and loudly.

(*Source:* James Joyce, *A Portrait of the Artist as a Young Man*, Cape, 1968)

THE COLLAPSE
OF THE IRISH
HOME RULE
PARTY

By 1891 Parnell was dead, and the Home Rule Party was without a leader. Gladstone's second Home Rule Bill was defeated by the House of Lords in 1892. O'Connell and Parnell had been unable to change the constitutional position of Ireland from within the British political system. The divisions created within Ireland and Britain remained unchanged. With Home Rule defeated, and a split in the Irish Party, a new group gradually formed called the Irish Parliamentary Party.

Why did the leaders of the Catholic Church condemn Parnell?

Do you think that the extract from the novel presents an exaggerated picture of the depth of people's feelings on this issue?

1900-1912

Irish affairs were moulded by more than British jurisdiction in the twentieth century. Events in Europe were moving towards the conflict of the First World War, and competition from Germany and America was having an effect on the British economy. Within Britain there was much civil unrest. A General Election in 1906 swept the Liberals to power. The Party maintained its support of Irish Home Rule, and in April 1912 the third Liberal Home Rule Bill was introduced.

In Ireland, social and intellectual movements thrived, rather than politics. There was an upsurge of interest in Ireland's Gaelic past. Literature and the theatre flourished, the Gaelic League revived the Celtic language, and the Gaelic Athletic Association drew a large membership. Both the Gaelic League and the GAA contained nationalist supporters who worked under cover of these organizations. The Sinn Féin (We ourselves) movement was founded by Arthur Griffiths in 1905, but, like other aspects of nationalist politics, remained without support. Slowly, the Irish party at Westminster grew again, under the guidance of John Redmond. By 1912 Redmond's party controlled the balance of power at Westminster, and agreed to support the Liberal Party in return for Home Rule. The Conservative Party pledged support for Ulster, the Protestants and the Orange Order.

THE ULSTER
VOLUNTEERS
AND THE IRISH
VOLUNTEER
FORCE

Ulster responded to the Home Rule threat by recruiting and training the Ulster Volunteers. Two hundred thousand Protestants signed a covenant against Home Rule. Many used their own blood. In some households in Ulster today, the covenants are kept on display to preserve the memory of this period in the history of Protestants. The Catholic response was to form the Irish Volunteer Force, and train a new group of Irish nationalists. Both sides drilled troops, marched and took to "gun running".

THE FIRST
WORLD WAR

The Home Rule Bill became law on 15 September 1914, but was never implemented. On 4 August 1914 Britain declared war on Germany. It was to last for four years. A special Cabinet was formed. Redmond, the leader of the Irish Nationalists at Westminster, was invited to join, but refused to do so. Carson, the leader of the Ulster Unionists, did join the War Cabinet. This gave the Unionists a strong political position in British politics. Ulster industry strengthened the Unionist cause further. Both Nationalists and Unionists supported Britain during the war years, and Redmond and Carson pledged support openly. Some Irish Nationalists, in particular those with IRB connections, refused to fight on the side of Great Britain.

FOR THE GLORY OF IRELAND

WILL YOU GO OR MUST I?

Why would recruitment posters use images of women in the campaign to enlist soldiers? Do you think this is an effective propaganda poster? Why do you think the Irish people gave more support to the British government than to the Nationalists?

Not all Nationalists agreed that they should be involved in a war on behalf of the British Empire. Nevertheless, about a quarter of a million Irish people fought in the armed forces in the war, and 60,000 Irish soldiers were killed.

THE EASTER RISING

Some republicans decided that the war gave them an opportunity for "direct action" in the tradition of the IRB, or in the cause of socialism. They decided on a separate plan which was to be a republican uprising. The action of the Irish in 1916 was to serve as an inspiration to other countries in their struggle for independence from Britain. A small group of republicans and socialists planned an uprising in Dublin, which was to take place on Bank Holiday Monday. Ireland was to be proclaimed a republic, Poblacht na hEireann, and a handout was printed.

The republicans took seven key sites in Dublin. The Post Office in Sackville Street was their headquarters. The British were taken by surprise, and had to move troops very quickly. On Tuesday, they sent for reinforcements, and by Wednesday these extra soldiers had arrived. The British troops were to place a cordon round the centre of Dublin and move in, fighting street by street until the rebel strongholds had been taken. By Wednesday, the British troops were in position. There were a thousand republicans in all, and the British troops outnumbered them by twenty to one.

On Wednesday the worst part of the fighting took place. The people of Dublin were not sure whether they should feel sympathy for the bravery of the republicans or hatred for those who had caused their city to be stormed and burned.

The British continued to tighten their cordon. Rebel strongholds were pounded by artillery and the army started fires so that barricades in the streets would be destroyed. The city of Dublin began to burn.

The leaders of the uprising had known that they would be defeated. They expected to lose their lives either as they defended their strongholds, or when they were captured by the British. Some now saw the necessity of surrender. Most wished to fight on. The decision to surrender was taken.

The Easter Rising is an event in Irish history that moved people deeply at the time. It is remembered with intensity today as well. Those who died, or were executed, were considered great heroes. One famous Irish poet, W.B. Yeats, put the republican case in his poem, "Easter 1916". A less well-known Irish poem gives a viewpoint from the memory of an Ulster child:

So reading the memoirs of Maud Gonne,
    Daughter of an English mother and a soldier father,
I note how a single purpose can be founded on
    A jumble of opposites:
Dublin Castle, the vice-regal ball,
    The embassies of Europe,
Hatred scribbled on a wall,
    Gaols and revolvers.
And I remember, when I was little, the fear
    Bandied among the servants
That Casement would land at the pier
    With a sword and a horde of rebels;
And how we used to expect, at a later date,
    When the wind blew from the west, the noise of shooting
Starting in the evening at eight
    In Belfast in the York Street district;
And the voodoo of the Orange bands
    Drawing an iron net through darkest Ulster,
Flailing the limbo lands—
    The linen mills, the long wet grass, the ragged hawthorn.
And one read black where the other read white, his hope
    The other man's damnation:

(*Source:* Louis MacNeice, "Autumn Journal" (xvi), *The Faber Book of Irish Verse*, ed. J. Montague, Faber and Faber, 1978)

Louis MacNeice spent most of his childhood in England. What images does he use to express his memories of his Belfast years?

Find out about Casement's involvement in the Easter Rising. Why did Ulster people fear his landing in Ireland?

What opposites does MacNeice give as examples of the division between Irish communities?

This chapter has traced the stormy history of Anglo-Irish relations in the nineteenth and early twentieth centuries. What particular problems had faced political leaders?

For what reasons had republicans and Orangemen chosen to use threats and violence, rather than constitutional methods, to gain political ends?

Conflict and Consequence

By 1917 Asquith's Liberal government in Britain had been replaced by a coalition under Lloyd George. Carson was a member of the coalition War Cabinet, and Ulster Unionists exerted a great deal of influence in politics at Westminster. Lloyd George established a new working party to discuss the implementation of the 1914 Home Rule Act, and it proposed an independent Ulster of six counties. However, the Nationalist Parliamentary Party would not agree that the partition of Ireland should be permanent, and the talks broke down. Outside Ulster, Sinn Féin members concentrated on building support for the Republican cause. They proposed that the new constitution for Ireland should state that there was to be "an independent Irish Republic". In the election of December 1918 they gained a massive victory. The Irish Parliamentary Party collapsed.

THE DÁIL EIREANN, 1919

On 21 January 1919 Sinn Féin MPs met in Dublin. They formally declared that they were opening a new parliament for Ireland, which was to be based in Dublin and not at Westminster. This new parliament was to be called Dáil Eireann, which in English means the Assembly of Ireland. The members of this assembly were to be known as Teachtaí, or deputies. In view of the large number of seats gained by Sinn Féin in the 1918 election, they felt justified in stating that the government of Ireland was to be republican.

Eamon de Valera was elected President of Dáil Eireann while he was still in prison in England. In February 1919 he was smuggled out of prison, and in June he went to America to raise funds. Arthur Griffith took the place of President of the Dáil in de Valera's absence. In Ireland, the IRA (formerly the IRB, until Easter 1916), under the leadership of Michael Collins, began to reorganize the republican campaign.

The republicans decided that if they were to win independence, they would have to take it for themselves. In August 1919, the Dáil and the IRA took a new oath which bound them to defend the Irish Republic against attack, and by September undeclared war was raging between the IRA and the British government.

THE IRA AND BRITISH REPRISALS

IRA resistance was based on local and regional groups. There was also a special squad which operated over the whole of the country, and carried out executions of British government agents and members of the Royal Irish Constabulary, the main British force. The IRA reprisals were so effective that RIC men resigned in large numbers. The British drafted in more men to help the RIC. The first recruits, wearing a mixture of RIC dark green uniform and army brown, became known as the Black and Tans. More officers were required, and these were formed into a new group called the Auxiliaries. Black and Tans and Auxiliaries operated under the authority of the British government, together with the RIC.

The first reinforcements arrived in Ireland in March 1920. This was to be the worst year as IRA attacks were followed by British reprisals, and

Ordinary people were forced to serve "two masters", as the IRA fought the British. In this photograph the Black and Tans have captured Sinn Féiners. Both sides acted ruthlessly, and reprisals took the form of burning houses and factories, and ambushes and shootings.

millions of pounds-worth of property went up in flames. The British authorities stated that for every one IRA attack, there would be two British reprisals. The death toll mounted, until Sunday, 21 November, when an IRA attack on 14 British officers was followed by a Black and Tan attack on an All Ireland Gaelic Football Final, in which 12 civilians died. "Bloody Sunday" was not the end of the campaign of violence, but it shook some members of the Dáil into contemplating negotiations with the British. A new Government of Ireland Act had been debated and passed by the British Parliament in 1920. Eamon de Valera left America for Ireland.

Elections were held in May 1921, as provided for under the Government of Ireland Act. The Unionists were given six counties, a parliament in Belfast, and home rule; and a partition separated those counties from the 26 counties which would be governed from Dublin. The IRA and the Dáil refused to accept partition, but took part in the election. Sinn Féin swept into power unopposed in 124 out of 128 of the new southern constituencies. In the north, the Ulster Unionists took 40 out of 52 seats.

By June 1921, the IRA were so short of supplies of ammunition that they had to resort to attacking property by the use of arson. King George V opened the new Northern Ireland Parliament and asked for peace. An acceptable solution had to be found. Ulster Unionists, British politicians and the IRA met in conferences for several months.

A DIVIDED ISLAND – THE ANGLO-IRISH TREATY, 1921

The following information has been taken from the clauses of the Anglo-Irish Treaty, 1921. It created two Irelands: one, in the north-east, contained six counties, where the Protestants were in an overall majority; the other 26 counties were to form a new Dominion called the Irish Free State. There were to be two parliaments, one in Belfast, the other in Dublin. The boundary line, or partition, was to be discussed by representatives from Britain, Northern Ireland and the Irish Free State at a later date. Ulster Unionists were given home rule, but with a difference! Under the treaty

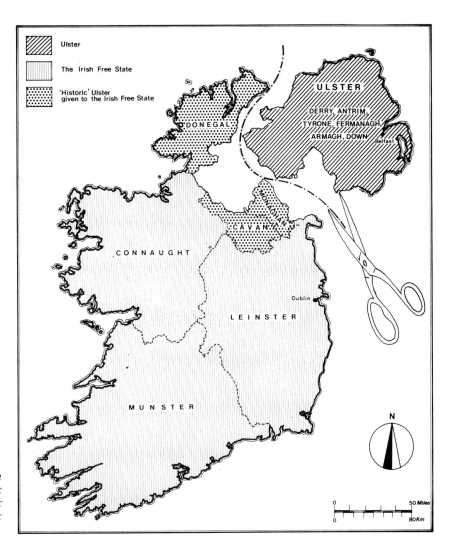

Ulster

The Irish Free State

'Historic' Ulster given to the Irish Free State

ULSTER

DERRY, ANTRIM, TYRONE, FERMANAGH, ARMAGH, DOWN

Belfast

DONEGAL

MONAGHAN

CAVAN

CONNAUGHT

LEINSTER

Dublin

MUNSTER

N

0   50 *Miles*
0   80 *Km*

A divided island: a Protestant Ulster of six counties and a Catholic Dominion of twenty-six counties.

they were allowed to petition the King of Britain to withdraw from any political connection with the rest of Ireland. After having battled against home rule for so long, they were persuaded to agree to it to prevent themselves from being ruled from Dublin. They could make a permanently separate Protestant state of Ulster. The republicans were threatened with a renewal of the war, and a full-scale British invasion within three days if they did not sign the treaty. There were many objections to the pressures which were applied by the British government.

"Historic" Ulster contained *nine* counties. The new Ulster contained Derry, Antrim, Tyrone, Fermanagh, Armagh and Down. The other three counties of Donegal, Monaghan and Cavan were put into the territory given to the Irish Free State.

The Anglo-Irish Treaty stated that southern Ireland should become a Dominion. This was a special political development which gave the new government independence and control over all internal law-making, while foreign policy, peace settlements and trade agreements were still controlled by the British government. Representatives of the Dominion went to Imperial Conferences in England.

Other countries which were Dominions at this time were Canada, South Africa, Australia and New Zealand. They had previously been colonies of white settlement, but now governed themselves. Each Dominion swore an oath of loyalty to the British Crown, and the Crown's representative, a Governor General, was sent to the Dominion. Ireland did not fit this pattern of Dominion. Nevertheless, becoming a Dominion was the only constitutional course to independence on offer to the Irish people in 1921.

Strong supporters of the republican cause and members of the IRA found it unacceptable that the political issue of Ireland's future should be settled in London. They were not prepared to swear an oath of loyalty to the British Crown, as this was directly opposite to republican ideas. There were heated debates in the Dáil, and the arguments were bitter and divisive. On 6 December 1921, the Anglo-Irish Treaty was signed by the Irish delegation in England. The Dáil had to ratify the treaty before a new government could take over the running of the country.

The Dáil voted to accept the Anglo-Irish Treaty on 7 January 1922. The Dáil was now suspended, and a provisional government ran the country until elections could take place later that year. Violence broke out on both sides of the border when the IRA refused to accept that this voting had been final. Anti-treaty IRA members fought against the new Free State's army and police force. The new leaders found themselves having to fight those who had been their allies before December 1921.

The first election of the Irish Free State was held in May 1922. The voters had to decide whether their votes would be cast for the Pro-Treaty Party, called Cumann na nGaedheal, or against it, for the rebel Sinn Féiners and the IRA. The results gave a victory to the Pro-Treaty Party. This election confirmed the existence of the Irish Free State, and the votes cast gave the people a real government, rather than a "paper" one.

A year of civil war followed. The Free State was determined to end republican violence and arrested IRA members throughout 1922 and 1923. The civil war left deep divisions within the new Dominion, and a great deal of bitterness. The republicans under de Valera surrendered their arms in April 1923, but did not surrender their cause. Other members of the IRA regrouped to fight again, or left Ireland for America.

On 6 December 1922, the Irish Free State replaced the provisional government, within the deadline of a year, which had been set by the treaty. On 7 December Ulster opted out from any political ties with the Irish Free State, and created a separate state for Protestants.

THE CONSTITUTION OF THE IRISH FREE STATE

The Dáil debated a new constitution for the Irish Free State. The Constitution, or Saorstát Eireann, became law in October 1922. It provided for a two-house legislature, the Dáil and the Seanad, or Senate. The Dáil was to be the house containing all elected members. The Seanad's members were to be partly elected by the Dáil and partly nominated by the Prime Minister. In order to protect the Protestant minority in the Irish Free State, the Prime Minister was directed to represent "minorities or interests not adequately represented in the Dáil. Also, a system of voting by proportional representation was put into effect. Members of the Dáil were elected on the basis of universal adult suffrage, in proportion to the number of people they represented. The size of the Dáil would vary according to the number in the population, but it was designed to be the most powerful part of the government, and the Seanad could not delay any Dáil legislation for any length of time. The Dáil also chose the Prime Minister, and the other leading ministers which he nominated required the agreement of the Dáil.

Under Dominion status, a representative of the British Crown, a Governor General, was formally recognized. His role was that of an unelected advisor, who assembled and dismissed Parliament. The presence of a Governor General, and the oath of loyalty to the Crown as the representative of the British Empire, kept the republicans out of the Dáil, and for four years they took no part in political life. The republicans were in the strange position of having achieved political power, but refusing to use it because of their principles. During these early years, there were so many problems with the IRA, and internal security, that when the Boundary Commission met to discuss the border, the Free State eventually agreed to abandon its claim to Ulster, in return for the British cancelling some debts which the Free State had undertaken to pay. The border became a permanent solution to the Ulster problem in 1925.

From 1923 to 1931 rapid changes took place within the British Empire, and the Irish Free State played an important role in bringing them about. Discussions began on the status of the Dominions. At the next Imperial Conference in 1926, Arthur Balfour produced a statement, which became the Statute of Westminster in 1931. This was not enough for the Irish republicans, some of whom chose to join Eamon de Valera's party, Fianna Fáil (Warriors of Ireland). In 1932 it won the election and de Valera headed the new government.

EAMON DE VALERA

In his history of Ireland, a modern historian, F.S.L. Lyons, has called Eamon de Valera "the constitutional Houdini of his generation"! Houdini was a famous nineteenth-century escapologist, who was particularly clever at getting out of handcuffs. Eamon de Valera is famous in the history of Irish republicanism for having worked out a plan for the Irish Free State to escape from its legal connections with Britain. Under his leadership the Dáil began to break the Anglo-Irish Treaty where it clashed with the sovereignty of the Irish Free State. By May 1933, the oath was removed, and the position of the Governor General had been made meaningless by substituting a British Governor General with a Fianna Fáil supporter, who "rubber-stamped" all decisions taken by the Dáil.

De Valera challenged the need to maintain any British connection. In his view, his country's history was more than British. Canada, South Africa, Australia and New Zealand were colonies of white settlement, which had been given independence peaceably. The Irish Free State had achieved independence through revolution, fighting for Gaelic freedom. When India gained independence in 1947, its constitutional development took the same pattern, and the Indian Parliament, the Lok Sabha, declared India a republic. Unlike Eire, India remained a member of the British Commonwealth of Nations.

EIRE

In 1937 a new constitution was made law. Eire (or Ireland) was the new name of the new state. The British Cabinet and the Dominions debated this change and accepted it. The British government then agreed to leave Eire altogether.

By the Anglo-Irish Treaty of 1921 Britain had kept some naval bases. In 1938 these ports were given back. Eire could now follow an independent foreign policy, and this began in 1939, when Eire declared neutrality during the Second World War. In 1948 the republican dream was finally realized when Poblacht na hEireann, the Republic of Ireland, came into existence. Soon afterwards the Republic left the Commonwealth. In 1949, the British government reaffirmed the position of Northern Ireland, and stated that any change in the political situation in Ulster could come into effect only with the consent of the majority there. The only issue left unresolved, as far as Eire is concerned, is the partition, its permanence, and the future for the Protestant nation in Ulster.

THE PROBLEM OF PARTITION

The partition of Ireland caused grave concern from the time the idea was first suggested. The boundary became a permanent settlement in 1925. During the Second World War the gulf between north and south widened, since the Republic of Eire was not involved and guarded its neutrality with care, while the Ulster Unionists suffered greatly. Today the Dáil still supports the cause of republicanism and unification, but the reality of the "Troubles", as they have been called in Ulster, would pose too much of a problem to handle by a simple transfer of power from Westminster to Dublin. Nevertheless, this continues to be the focus of political dreams.

There are other areas which cause concern. De Valera's new constitution of 1937 stressed the basic freedoms and rights of citizens in Eire. The constitution guaranteed each citizen the rights of equality in law, politics and religion. Articles 41 to 44 deal with the family, education, private property and religion. The Catholic Church has a special position in the constitution, as the religion followed by the majority of Eire's citizens. The family clauses in the constitution reflect Catholic attitudes towards the role of women, and abortion, contraception and divorce are not allowed. Strict censorship is maintained by the state, in books, films, periodicals and magazines. There have been many changes in such attitudes over recent years because of the influence of the mass media in the Republic. Nevertheless, Ulster Protestants find these Catholic values unacceptable. This remains one of the most difficult areas to solve.

ULSTER DRUMS

The following extract is from a novel called *Under Goliath*, which is set in Ulster and tells the story of Catholic and Protestant lives through a Protestant boy called Alan. Alan explains his wish to play a drum, and his thoughts about his Protestant history:

When I was young and a Belfast boy I took it into my head to play a drum, thus making myself a curse to the neighbours and the world at large. But it was not your piddling side-drum I wanted to bang but the war-drum of Ulster, the lambeg.

Now there is what you might call a drum: five feet across and three wide, made from the skins of a dozen lambs stretched on a circle of oak, painted with the heads of heroes, and bound with silver struts. When you pound on that you use canes four feet long, and as it throbs the panes in your windows rattle, pots fall off the shelf, doors shake, and the false teeth clatter in old men's heads. It has a call that would stop your heart from beating – and maybe your mind from thinking...

At any rate, I got the yearning for the drum and so, on my thirteenth birthday, I went down to the Old Sash Lodge of the Loyal Order of United Orangemen and proposed myself as a member of Mr Mackracken's drum and fife Walking Band.

Now in case you think that the Orangemen are maybe a body of greengrocers or whatever, let me tell you they are no such thing. They are so called after William of Orange, a Dutchman who became King of England. He was a very ardent Protestant king who came to Ireland in the year 1690 and gave the Catholics a terrible beating at the Battle of the Boyne. To keep the memory of that beating alive, and to make sure that the Protestant religion stays on top of the league in Northern Ireland, is what the Orange Order is all about, although it's even money whether most of its members know as much about religion as you do.

(*Source:* Peter Carter, *Under Goliath*, Puffin, 1977)

In this picture you can see an Orange supporter beating a lambeg drum, as he marches with an Orange Lodge procession. The Orange Order unites Protestants from all classes, whether rich or poor. This march is part of the 12 July celebrations. In Northern Ireland religious and political ideas become focused in celebrations of important anniversaries. (The photograph comes from an Ulster newspaper, The Ulster Star.)

Here, in another extract from "Autumn Journal" by Louis MacNeice, is his childhood memory of Ulster drums.

Drums on the haycock, drums on the harvest, black
   Drums in the night shaking the windows:
King William is riding his white horse back
   To the Boyne on a banner.
Thousands of banners, thousands of white
   Horses, thousands of Williams
Waving thousands of swords and ready to fight
   Till the blue sea turns to orange.

(*Source:* Louis MacNeice, "Autumn Journal" (xvi), *The Faber Book of Irish Verse*, ed. J. Montague, Faber and Faber, 1978)

The extract from Under Goliath *gives a sense of the excitement felt by a young child learning to play a part in adult society. Do you feel that the poem has this same feeling of excitement?*

Learning to play the drums for the Orange Order marches is part of growing up for Protestants in Ulster. Children learn on small drums, and progress onto large ones, until they are chosen to march in a parade as a lambeg drummer. Drumming practices, and competitions for drumming places in the marches, are frequent, and go on for many hours without stopping. Long canes are used to beat the drums. Practice sessions are so lengthy that hands can become raw and bleed. The beat of the drums is a triumphant sound to Protestants, but an ominous one to Catholics. It represents both the past and the present history of Ulster Protestantism.

ULSTER   Drawing a boundary line separating the six counties of Ulster from the Irish Free State gave the Protestants a political majority in Ulster in 1921. A parliament was set up which was allowed a limited form of self-government, appropriate to a situation in which the majority had decided to keep rule from Westminster. This was accepted reluctantly because there was no political alternative other than being ruled by the Dáil from Dublin. On 7 December 1922 Ulster followed this separatist policy, and opted out of further political connection with the Irish Free State. The Unionist Party won the general election in 1921, with an overwhelming majority. This was to continue to be the pattern of political life in Ulster, with no fewer than 40 out of 52 seats in the Belfast parliament held by supporters of the Ulster Union.

From the beginning, Ulster politics reflected the tension between the two communities living there, and the unresolved problems between the two states. When the Irish Free State voted in the new constitution and became a republic, the Unionists were determined that their state should remain independent. The Ulster Unionists were also convinced that the only way to achieve stability was to maintain their power in Stormont, their parliament, and in local councils. It is considered essential that Ulster Unionists are members of the Orange Order. This is a well-organized movement that attracts Protestants from all classes and social backgrounds. The Ulster Unionist Party remained in a majority from 1921 to 1972, virtually unopposed in Stormont.

In local government the Unionists maintained control through giving votes based on ownership of property. The reason behind this was simply that those who paid rates should have representation on the local council, and vote. Voting was based on owning houses, paying rent or owning businesses. Many Catholics were unable to vote because they did not fit in these categories. They were caught in a "vicious circle" from which they could not break out. Ulster remained the only part of the United Kingdom which maintained this sort of discrimination. In addition, businesses were also allowed to nominate up to six council members each and vote as well. This system of plural voting was eventually abolished in 1968, but these reforms came too late to relieve the growth of tension within the separate communities of Ulster.

Much of the fear about Ulster Catholics can be traced back to the terrible years of the civil war. Some sense of this feeling is captured in another extract from *Under Goliath*. Alan has joined his brother Billy in the pub, and listens to an argument between Billy and their Uncle Jack.

'I'm no bigot.' Jack was angry.

'I didn't say you were,' Billy answered.

'I'll shake the hand of any man.'

'All right.'

'I will,' Jack said, as if someone had denied it.

Billy nodded. 'You're in the Orange Order though, aren't you?'

'I am that. I am that,' Jack said. 'I'm a Loyalist. This country is part of Britain and I want it to stay that way. I don't want to become part of the Republic of Ireland, and that's a fact. I'm for the Queen and the Protestant cause and I'm for the Border. I want it to stay there. What's wrong with that?"

Billy didn't answer that. Instead he leaned forward. 'You're in the Bs too, aren't you?'

'That I am,' Jack said. 'I know my duty.'

'O.K.' Billy seemed to agree with him. He leaned forward. 'You've got two votes, haven't you?'

'Hey, hey,' Jack pushed his cup away. 'What are you getting at?'

Billy spoke without any expression in his voice at all. 'You've got two votes. One for your house and one for your shop. This is the only place in Britain where a man can have two votes. That's all.'

Jack looked a bit puzzled. He opened his mouth as if to speak, then closed it again. . . .

He put his big oilskin on and went to the door. He opened it and turned and his face was dark and frightening.

'Let met tell *you* something, Billy,' he said. 'You're a clever lad, right enough, but I've seen the time when a man could open the door on a street like this and get shot down like a dog. You don't remember those times but I do. I saw the I.R.A. come over the Border and declare war on this province. . . . But they're not going to bomb Ulster into the Republic and, by Jesus, if they try we'll give them a hiding like we did the last time.'

(*Source:* Peter Carter, *Under Goliath*, Puffin Books, 1977)

In this passage Uncle Jack explains his viewpoint as a "son of Ulster". You will understand this last reference more clearly if you look back at the photograph showing an Orange march and a lambeg drum. His viewpoint is based on four beliefs. What are they?

In 1922, a Special Powers Act was passed in Ulster. One of the things it did was to create a part-time police force, the B Specials, whose job was to support the full-time police force, the Royal Ulster Constabulary. Uncle Jack is in the Bs. What does he mean when he refers to this as a "duty"?

A modern Irish historian has interpreted the situation in Ulster in a slightly different way. What he says is difficult to understand. He tries to explain the divisions which have grown as a result of migration patterns and settlement.

The Ulsterman carries the map . . . of religious geography in his mind almost from birth. He knows which villages, which roads and streets, are Catholic, or Protestant, or 'mixed'. It not only tells him where he can, or cannot, wave an Irish tricolour or wear his Orange sash, but imposes on him a complex behaviour pattern and a special way of looking at political problems.

(*Source:* A.T.Q. Stewart, *The Narrow Ground. Aspects of Ulster 1609-1969*, Faber and Faber, 1977)

Can you trace the history of religious geography through migration and settlement in Ulster in other chapters of this book?

Under Goliath is an imaginary account of the kinds of real events which we see reported on the news. Compare the extracts from it with this account by an historian:

No one who has been caught in a Belfast riot against his will is likely to regard it as one of the higher forms of human activity. . . . Stone throwing, for example, is a military art of considerable sophistication and great antiquity.... That simple fact has determined the image of Ulster most frequently presented to the world – that of well-armed soldiers and police cowering behind armoured cars and street corners under a hail of bricks and stones. These soldiers might as well be Roman legionaries, for all the good their modern weapons are; their only protection is a shield, a steel helmet and a visor. Schoolboys can dance right up to the armoured vehicles and launch a brick or a nail bomb with deadly accuracy.

(*Source:* A.T.Q. Stewart, *The Narrow Ground. Aspects of Ulster 1609-1969*, Faber and Faber Ltd, 1977)

Do you think that A.T.Q. Stewart is right when he says that the most frequent view of Ulster shown on television is of violence?

How is it possible for stone throwers to be so successful against well-armed troops?

This photograph was taken in the Bogside (Catholic) area of Londonderry in 1969. Civil rights demonstrations had taken place. British people take this sort of picture of Ulster for granted. We are quite used to seeing this on our television screens. Do you think other countries might judge us harshly when they see scenes like this on their televisions?

This picture was taken in the Falls Road area of Belfast. What will this Ulster child learn as he grows up, about the society in which he lives? The process of growing up is sometimes called socialization. What pressures might persuade children to adopt violent behaviour? Will children find it easy to break out of the pattern of Ulster politics?

A.T.Q. Stewart writes that this art of stone throwing is very old. Perhaps he is referring to the Bible story of David and Goliath. If he is, who won that battle?

Catholics asked for changes in voting, housing rights and in local government. From what you have read so far, would you say that they were justified in their demands?

Both communities in Ulster feel threatened by the past, and for this reason respond to the political situation with deep emotion. The Protestants feel strongly committed to the connection with Britain, and wish to remain British citizens. During the Second World War Ulster played an important role on Britain's side, and loyalty to the Crown, and to Britain, remains unchanged. Ulster Protestants feel a sense of patriotism, and support the connection which makes them a part of the United Kingdom. Catholics are less supportive because they feel second-class citizens. The communities live separate lives, and often learn two entirely different versions of Irish history through their churches, their youth organizations and their schools.

Do you think that all Ulster children grow up feeling strong religious ties with their communities?

Can you see separate histories reflected within this book?

Do you think it is possible to teach, or write, accounts of historical events without showing a cultural bias?

CIVIL RIGHTS FOR CATHOLICS

Catholic reaction to Protestant authority is based on demands for better housing conditions, better jobs and equal political rights. Another Catholic complaint was that the Special Powers Act and the B Specials were used to discriminate against Catholics. There are few Catholics who wished to serve either in the B Specials, or now, in the Royal Ulster Constabulary. The Civil Rights Movement in Ulster grew quickly during 1968 and 1969. During the week of 12-19 August 1969, rioting began which lasted two days. This was shown on national and international television. For the first time the British public was faced with the reality of the tension in Ulster. Some political reforms were being attempted, but these came too late to prevent both communities from hardening their attitudes. In 1969 and 1970 the clashes between the communities occurred during the months of "historic" provocation. From 1971 the violence was not contained in the usual months. British troops began to be drafted in from 1970 to maintain a peace-keeping exercise in Ulster. To Catholics this was another provocative move, and they began to react against the troops in Ulster. The IRA supported the Civil Rights campaign, but split into two groups over how best to obtain Catholic rights. One group of IRA members maintained the traditional republican approach, and the new group, the Provisional IRA, or "Provos", decided to step up the use of political violence and direct action, both in Ulster and in mainland Britain. The use of violence has further widened sectarian differences.

In response to the paramilitary organizations of the IRA and the Provos, the Protestants have formed the Ulster Volunteer Force, the UVF, and the Ulster Defence Association, the UDA. A new Protestant party has been formed, called the Democratic Unionist Party, and it is supported by both moderate Protestants and extremists. Sinn Féin continues its tradition of being the political arm of the IRA. The Social and Democratic Labour Party attracts most Catholic support, and provides an alternative political platform. Living with the reality of sectarian differences has not been easy since the upsurge of violence from 1969.

INTERNMENT From 1971 more troops were sent from Britain to Ulster, and as the situation seemed to be rapidly moving out of control the British government agreed to the use of internment. Under a new law introduced in August 1971, the Ulster government could arrest and imprison anyone suspected of terrorist activity. By now Catholics were completely estranged from the Ulster government, and increasingly anti-army because of the introduction of CS gas. Catholics were arrested in large numbers, and were subjected to various kinds of torture which involved loss of sleep, loss of food and disorientation techniques. In retaliation the internees and prisoners have used hunger strikes and excrement smearing as weapons, as well as methods of terrorism.

DIRECT RULE FROM WESTMINSTER Since 1972 Northern Ireland has been under direct rule of the Westminster Parliament, and Stormont has been suspended. This has happened because there was no agreement between the political parties in Ulster, and the Unionists had obviously lost control of the political situation. The Royal Ulster Constabulary and the British Army are the front-line forces in the peace-keeping exercise in Ulster. The RUC, the police force, have a reputation for taking a hard line against Catholics, and this reputation has not disappeared since the disbanding of the B Specials in 1969. The armed forces are not trained in the work they have to do in Ulster and are forced to handle situations for which they are not qualified. A plebiscite held in 1973 voted to keep the political connection with Great Britain. Many Catholics refused to vote on this issue. Over 8,000 separate terrorist attacks have taken place since then.

ANGLO-IRISH TALKS BETWEEN LONDON AND DUBLIN, 1984

Britain is committed to maintaining the status quo in Ulster. However, the upsurge of violence created a situation where talks between Britain and the Republic of Eire were put into effect in 1984. In 1985 they agreed to cooperate over border security, the restriction of terrorism and policing. Ulster Protestants have reacted strongly against the moves towards consultation between Dublin and Westminster, and have rejected the right of the British government to do this.

Ultimate responsibility for affairs in Ulster is held by the British government, and the maintenance of law and order, and the protection of all the citizens who live there, is under the control of Westminster. Any political change which occurs has to have the consent of the British Parliament, and the support of all political parties. The Anglo-Irish Agreement was welcomed by all the leaders of the British political parties. The Ulster Unionists were the main opponents.

ON REFLECTION:

Historians study the events which have shaped the past. In the discussions about the future of Northern Ireland the following suggestions have been raised at various times over the past few years. Do you think any of these suggestions would be successful?

To limit the activities of republican terrorists, and to unify Ireland, Britain could pass a law through the Westminster Parliament, which would give responsibility for the government of Ulster to the Republic of Eire. This would reunify the whole of Ireland, and give the Dáil full control. This has been rejected by Ulster Protestants.

An alternative to this might be a permanent settlement of the present political situation, with the Westminster Parliament ruling directly. This would involve the continued presence of large numbers of troops to provide a peace-keeping force, and would lead to an upsurge in republican terrorism.

Ulster could be given independence and complete sovereignty. This has only been offered to states which could prove that they were financially self-sufficient. Ulster would find this difficult to prove.

Britain could ask for the intervention of the United Nations, and propose the introduction of an international peace-keeping force to be stationed in Northern Ireland. This suggestion, first made in 1969, has not received a great deal of consideration.

A STATE OF SIEGE

Whatever the outcome, it is no longer the physical presence of a border between the Republic and Ulster which dominates the present situation, nor religion which causes the greatest divide. It is, perhaps, the "siege mentality" which has developed in both Catholic and Protestant minds, that affects the decision-making, and will be the hardest problem to solve.

Cage under siege

This is home. This is the Irish North.
Where we endure the earth's falling away
Rivets an iron sky to north and west.
Where the covetous South darkens, granite
Rears a grave wall. Eastward the sea recoils
Toward England, breathless with horror, sobs back.

On our borders the known world ends sheer.
We've pulled the sea around us like a shawl
And heaved the mountains higher. The waiting
South's bog-barbarians starve against a grand
Squiggle on our map. The sky is closed.
This is home. This is the Irish North.

(*Source:* Poem by Patrick Williams, quoted in *History File*, a BBC Radio and Television booklet, 1985)

ON REFLECTION:

Have the "in-depth" reporting and the influence of the mass media encouraged the use of violence as an acceptable method of political action?

Are we so accustomed to the use of force that we have discounted the consequences for the people of Ulster?

Do you think that violence and direct action have kept the issue of Ulster alive in the minds of the people of Britain?

What alternatives are there to the use of terrorism as a weapon for political change?

A women's movement for peace was begun in 1976. In what ways would women perceive the political situation in Ulster differently from men?

Are there other views of Ireland which are not represented in the media, or offered as alternatives within this book?

What do you see as the outcome of eight hundred years of Anglo-Irish relations?

Glossary

Act of Union (1800)	officially joined Ireland to England, so that Ireland was ruled by the Westminster Parliament.
agrarian societies	groups of Irish people wanting changes in landholding.
Anglo-Irish	of both English and Irish background.
Anglo-Irish Treaty (1921)	gave Dominion Status to Southern Ireland (Irish Free State) and limited rule to Ulster.
Auxiliaries	officers drafted into Ireland during the Civil War, 1919-22.
B Specials	a citizen force set up in Ulster to work with the Police Force. Serving citizens were usually Protestant.
Black and Tans	soldiers who served as an emergency British force, during the Civil War.
Brehon Laws	laws made by Gaelic judges for their society.
Catholic Association	an organization run by Daniel O'Connell in the early nineteenth century and which fought to get the vote for Catholics.
Catholic emancipation	freedom for Catholics to vote in the same way as Protestants.
cottier	an Irish tenant farmer.
Dáil Eireann	the Parliament of the Republic of Eire.
Druids	priests and sun worshippers.
Dublin Castle	the name given to the British administration of Ireland.
Eire	in English, All Ireland; under the 1937 Constitution, the new name for the Irish Free State.
English Pale	the area controlled by the English in Ireland from Norman to Tudor times.
Fenians (1858)	members of the IRB, named after Finn MacCool's soldiers.
Gaels	Iron age people who settled in Ireland, and gave Ireland its first culture.
Home Rule	limited self government for Ireland. Britain was left in charge of foreign affairs, trade and Empire.
Home Rule Party	founded in 1870 by Isaac Butt and led by Parnell. It collapsed after his death.
Irish Free State	the Dominion created by the Anglo-Irish Treaty, 1921, excluding Ulster.
Irish Republican Army (**IRA**) (1917)	the republican forces who fought against Britain during the Civil War. They oppose partition today.
Irish Republican Brotherhood (IRB) (1858)	republican emigrants, whose aim was to establish a republic by force.
Irish Volunteers (1913)	Catholics from the IRB who formed a military group against the Protestant Ulster Volunteers.
internment	the arrest and imprisonment without trial of terrorists in Ulster, 1970.
land leagues	*see* agrarian societies.
Land War	fought in the eighteenth and nineteenth centuries by tenants and agrarian societies against landowners and the British Army.
Nationalist Parliamentary Party	the Irish Home Rule Party, after the death of Parnell.
New English	settlers in Ireland, from England and Scotland, from the sixteenth century.
Old English	settlers in Ireland, from the time of the Norman Conquest to the sixteenth century.
Orange Order	a Protestant group, supporting William of Orange, founded in 1795.
plantation colony	a group of migrants, settled in another country by an official scheme.
Poblacht na hEireann	in English, the Republic of Ireland.

Protestant Ascendancy	the term used in the late seventeenth and eighteenth centuries for the rule of the landed Protestant class in Ireland.
Provos	the shortened term for the splinter group, the Provisional IRA.
Saorstát Eireann	the constitution of the Republic of Eire.
Seanad	the Senate of the Dáil.
sectarian	religious.
siege mentality	the term used to describe how Ulster Protestants feel about Ulster, and its relationship to the Republic of Eire.
Sinn Féin (1905)	founded by Arthur Griffith, to win independence for Ireland, through political means.
Social Democratic and Labour Party	the socialist party in Ulster.
Special Powers Act (1922)	an act passed by the Ulster government to suppress IRA activities.
Stormont	the Ulster Parliament.
Taoiseach	the leader of the government of the Irish Republic.
Tara	the land belonging to the Gaelic High King of All Ireland.
Teachtai	Irish deputies serving in the Dáil.
tuatha	an area controlled by a Gaelic chieftain, and the kinship group.
Ulster	historically nine provinces in the north-east of Ireland; now (since 1972) six provinces ruled separately from the Republic of Eire, by Westminster.
Ulster Unionists	supporters of the union between Ireland and England and opposers of Parnell's Home Rule Party.
Ulster Volunteer Force (1912-14)	Protestants who resisted Home Rule.
woodkerne	Gaelic footsoldiers, or mercenaries serving as footsoldiers in the Gaelic army.

Sources

Sources for School Students

This history book covers a wide range of Irish history, and travels back in time through many years. It may be difficult to find the connections in the book. You may wish to develop an interest in one particular period. One easier way to understand history is to read novels. Here are some titles you might like to select from your library shelves:
J. Johnstone, *Shadows on Our Skin* (Hamish Hamilton, 1977); P.J. Kavanagh, *Scarf Jack* (Puffin, 1980); P. Carter, *Under Goliath* (Puffin, 1977) (this novel also has a *Workbook*, published by the *Inner London Education Authority's English Centre*); D. Rees, *Green Bough of Liberty* (Dobson, 1980); J. Lingard, *The Twelfth Day of July* and *Across the Barricades* (Puffin, 1973).

Irish people are famous for writing poetry, plays and novels. Here are some famous names to follow back in time: stories of Celts and legends told by the Gaels, some of which are in translation from Gaelic; J. Swift, R.B. Sheridan, O. Goldsmith, T. Davis, P. Kearney, J. Joyce, O. Wilde, J.M. Synge, W.B. Yeats, G.B. Shaw, R. Graves, L. MacNeice, A. Cronin, E. O'Brien, S. Heaney, M. Binchey, S. Becket.

Finding out about Irish art is easy if you begin to look at large art books with big colour pictures. You should find these as reference books in your school library, and in your local library. You could ask your art teacher to help you begin a research project on Celtic design.

There are many other history books to read, some of which include short extracts from primary sources to help you understand how people felt in the past. There are many books on Northern Ireland or Ulster. Fewer books have been published on Eire. Here are some titles you might like to select from your library shelves:
J. Hewitt, *Talking about Northern Ireland* (Wayland, 1980) and *The Irish Question*, (1976); J. Hawthorne (ed.), *Two Centuries of Irish History* (BBC, 1966); S.R. Gibbons (ed.), *Ireland 1780-1914* (Blackie & Son, 1978); Schools Council Project 13-16, *The Irish*

Question (H. McDougall, 1977); O. Woodward, *Divided Island* (Heinemann, 1976); *Then and There, The Potato Famine and the Irish Emigrant* (Longman, 1976) and *The Easter Rising and Irish Independence* (1979); D. Bleakley, *Peace in Ulster* (Mowbray, 1972); N. Grant, *The Easter Rising* (Watts, 1972); N. Harris, *The Easter Rising* (Dryad Press, 1987); J. Nichol (ed.), *The Irish Question* (Macdonald, 1985).

The BBC Radio Service for Schools often produces programmes on Irish history and publishes booklets. There are many documentary programmes on television which will provide you with current information. In order to understand the information given, some general knowledge is necessary, so that you have a clear understanding of historical issues. The book titles provided here will give you interesting and informative general knowledge. Museums and art galleries, as well as the mass media, will help you with visual source material, and the Irish Tourist service is always helpful.

Many children you meet will have Irish families. Some of your teachers will be Irish. You may not know this, because they don't "sound" Irish. Sometimes they have deliberately lost their accents because they were teased about being Irish at school. If you have Irish friends, you may like to interview their families, and record their stories. Oral history is very important in Irish families, and you will be carrying on a special tradition, as well as learning historical skills. When you record their views of their history, you will understand how important it is to weigh all sorts of evidence, with care and understanding.

Sources for Senior Students and Teachers

Early Irish History

M. and L. de Paor, *Early Christian Ireland* (London, 1978)
J.K.S. St Joseph, *The Early Development of Irish Society* (Cambridge, 1969)
F.H.A. Aalen, *Man and the Landscape in Ireland* (London, 1978)

Medieval and Tudor History

T.W. Moody, F.X. Martin and F.J. Byrne, *A New History of Ireland. Vol. III* (Oxford, 1976)
J.F. Lydon, *The Lordship of Ireland in the Middle Ages* (Dublin, 1972)
R. Dudley Edwards, *Ireland in the Age of the Tudors* (London, 1977)
Grenfell Morton, *Elizabethan Ireland* (London, 1971)

Stuart and Georgian History

A.T.Q. Stewart, *The Narrow Ground. Aspects of Ulster 1609-1969* (London, 1977)
T.W. Moody, *The Ulster Question 1603-1973* (Dublin and Cork, 1974)
R.B. McDowell, *Ireland in the Age of Imperialism and Revolution 1760-1801* (Oxford, 1979)
W.E.A. Lecky, *History of Ireland in the Eighteenth Century* (London, 1892)

Nineteenth- and Twentieth-Century History

T. Desmond Williams, *Secret Societies in Ireland* (Dublin, 1973)
G.O. Tuathaigh, *Ireland before the Famine 1798-1848* (Dublin, 1974)
F.S.L. Lyons, *Ireland Since the Famine* (London, 1973)
N. Mansergh, *The Irish Question, 1840-1921* (London, 1965)
L.P. Curtis Jr, *Apes and Angels: The Irishman in Victorian Caricature* (Newton Abbot, 1971)
J.A. Murphy, *Ireland in the Twentieth Century* (Dublin, 1976)
R. Kee, *The Green Flag* (London, 1972)
D.W. Harkness, *The Restless Dominion* (Dublin, 1969)
J. Carty, *Ireland, a Documentary Record. 3 Vols.* (Dublin, 1949)
The Gill History of Ireland, II Vols. (Dublin, 1972 and 1975)
T.D. Williams and R.D. Edwards, *The Great Famine* (Dublin, 1956)
C. Woodham-Smith, *The Great Hunger* (London, 1962)
O.D. Edwards, *The Sins of Our Fathers: Roots of Conflict in Northern Ireland* (Dublin, 1970)
B. Kennelly (ed.), *The Penguin Book of Irish Verse* (London, 1970)
J. Montague (ed.), *The Faber Book of Irish Verse* (London, 1974)
K. Hoagland (ed.), *1000 Years of Irish Poetry* (New York, 1947)
A.T. Lucas, *Treasures of Ireland* (Dublin, 1973)

Current articles on Irish history are published in the journal *Irish Historical Studies*, available in specialist libraries and reference sections throughout the UK.

Timeline

PERIOD	DATES	IRELAND
Prehistoric **The religions of Shinto, Hinduism, Buddhism and Judaism**	**Until c. 43 AD** (All dating is approximate at this time in history.)	Ireland invaded across land bridge from Scotland. **6700 BC** Ireland becomes an island. **3500 BC** Hunters and gatherers become farmers. Stone Age migrants arrive. **2000-700 BC** Bronze Age migrants arrive. **700 BC** Iron Age Celts (Gaels) arrive. Tara established. Family life based on kinship groups.
The age of Greece, Rome and India **The religions of Christianity**	(Dating becomes more reliable because of written texts.)	Oral history passes on the great sagas. Brehon laws organize Celtic tribes. Gaelic life established. **432 AD** St Patrick begins conversion to Christianity. The Age of Gold. **795 AD** Viking raids and invasions. **1014 AD** Brian Boru killed at the battle of Clontarf.
The medieval world	**1066-1485** (**c. 1454** Handwritten texts are printed.)	**1070** Normans invade. The Pale established as Old English settlers move to Ireland. Anglo-Norman rule begins. **1366** Statutes of Kilkenny.
The early modern world **The age of Turkey** **Spain** **France** **and India** (continued on pages 70-71)	 1453 1496 1515 1556	**1494** Poyning's Law. **1536** Henry VIII Supreme Head of the Church in Ireland. Surrender and Regrant. Gaelic customs forbidden. **1553-58** First English colonization schemes. **1580** Famine in Munster. **1595** The Earl of Tyrone rebels. **1603** Earl of Tyrone surrenders to Elizabeth I. **1607** The Flight of the Earls. Land confiscated by England. **1608** Plantation schemes extended New English settlers move in.

ENGLAND/GREAT BRITAIN	CIVILIZATIONS & EMPIRES	EVENTS
England, Wales and Scotland invaded across land bridge from north Europe. **4500 BC** England, Wales and Scotland become an island. **700 BC** Celts (Brythoni) arrive.	**c. 4000 BC** Indus. **c. 3500 BC** Sumer. **c. 3100 BC** Egypt. **c. 2205 BC** China. **c. 1450** Minoan. **c. 538 BC** Persia. **c. 499 BC** Greece expands. **c. 275 BC** Rome expands. **c. 274 BC** Ashoka (India). **c. 110 BC** China expands.	Ice sheets melt away. People begin to move. **c. 3100 BC** Picture writing. Trading begins. **c. 2700 BC** Pyramids built. **c. 2200BC** Pen and ink writing. **c. 1500 BC** Aryans move from Central Asia. **c. 1400 BC** Hindu religion ideas written down. **c. 480 BC** Buddha dies. **c. 4 AD** Jesus born.
43 AD Invasion by Roman Army. **60 AD** Boudica leads rebellion against Rome. **367 AD** Raids and invasions by Angles and Saxons. **795 AD** Viking raids and invasions. **1016 AD** Canute King of England.	**227 AD** Persia. **320 AD** Gupta (India). **410 AD** Rome sacked. **800 AD** A Holy Roman Empire in Europe under Charlemagne. **900 AD** Chola (South India).	**c. 476** Roman Empire in the east stays. **c. 570** The Prophet (Islam) born. **c. 980** Vikings reach Greenland and travel on to America.
1066 AD Normans invade. **1086** Domesday Book records the pattern of landholding. **1154** Plantagenet succession. **1284** Wales conquered by England. **1338** England and France at war. **1458** Tudor succession. Henry VII takes the throne at Bosworth Field.	**c. 1237** Mongols expand in Central Asia. **c. 1325** Madi (North West Africa). **c. 1363** Tamerlaine conquers Asia.	**1099** Europeans go to war against the Muslim world. Overland journies to the east begin. **c. 1453** Turks capture Constantinople. Roman Empire in the east collapses.
1534 Henry VIII becomes Head of the Church in England. **1558** Elizabeth Tudor monarch of England and Wales. **1562-1603** Anglo-Irish Wars. **1558** Spain launches Armada and it is defeated. **1603** Stuart succession. **1610** Increasing conflict between King and Parliament.	**1493** Songhai. **1520** Turkey. **1526** Mughals invade India. **1556** Akbar of India extends his empire. **1603** Shogun takes control in Japan. **1609** Holland founding an eastern trading empire. **1613** Russia and the Romanovs.	**1492** Columbus explores the West Indies and discovers America. **1494** Europeans divide the world between Spain and Portugal. **1517** Christians become Protestants as well as Catholics. **1519** Magellan sails round the world. **1600** Conflict grows over European trade in the east and west.

Timeline

PERIOD	DATES	IRELAND
The early modern world (continued)		**1641** The Old English lead a Catholic uprising. **1649** Cromwell lands in Ireland. **1650** To Hell, Connaught, or West Indian slavery. Land confiscated by England. **c. 1688** The Siege of Derry. **1690** William of Orange defeats James II. Land confiscated by England. Penal Laws introduced.
The widening world **The age of France and Britain** **Industrialization, nationalism and imperialism**	1715-1880	**1775** Grattan and his parliament win temporary freedom from Britain. **1790s** Unrest in Ireland, both agrarian and political. **1795** Orange Order founded. **1796** Wolfe Tone and Bantry Bay. Troops sent from England. **1800** Act of Union. **1803** Emmet's rebellion. **1823** O'Connell founds the Catholic Association. **1843** Monster Meetings for repeal of the Union. **1845-49** The Great Starvation. **1848** Young Irelanders' rebellion and English coercion. Troops sent from England. **1858** The IRB founded to fight for freedom. **1871** Butt founds the Irish Home Rule League. **1875** Parnell enters Parliament. **1879** Famine, evictions and Land League. **1879-82** Land War and Parnell scandal. **1885/6** Riots in Belfast.
The modern world in the twentieth century **The rise of Fascism and Communism** **Superpowers** **The age of America and Russia** **Capitalism and Communism**	1900 to the present day 1950 to the present	**1909** Changes in landholding. **1912** Ulster Covenant. Illegal drilling. **1913** Volunteers formed. **1916** Easter Rising. **1918** Sinn Féin victories. Dáil opened. Guerilla warfare begins. IRA campaigns. **1921** Truce. **1921** Anglo-Irish Treaty creates the Irish Free State. **1921-23** Civil War. **1926** Fianna Fáil founded by de Valera. **1927** Fianna Fáil enters the Dáil. **1937** New constitution of Eire. **1939** Eire neutral in Second World War. **1948** Fine Gael and Clann na Poblachta enter Dáil. **1949** Eire a republic. Social issues take precedence in the Dáil. Eire leaves the Commonwealth. **1985** Anglo-Irish Treaty, Dublin/Westminster.

ENGLAND/GREAT BRITAIN	CIVILIZATIONS & EMPIRES	EVENTS
1642 Civil war begins. **1649** King executed and a Cromwellian Republic. **1688** The Catholic James II deposed. William and Mary become joint sovereigns. **1690 onwards** English at war against France. Navigation Acts. **1707** Scotland and England united. **1714** Hanoverian succession maintains Protestant rule in England. Georgian era begins.	**1630** Sweden and Gustavus Adolphus. **1659** France leading European nation. Wars on mainland Europe. **1713** Defeat of Louis XIV.	**1652** Cape Colony (Africa) founded by the Dutch. **1713** Treaty of Utrecht. Colonies taken by Europeans from countries out of Europe. Slave trade passed to Britain.
1759-63 The Seven Years War and a year of major victories. **1777-82** Britain fights America. **1790** Repressive government and wars against France. **1800** Act of Union. **1807** Slave Trade stopped. **1815** Napoleon defeated. Repression continues. **1829** Catholic Emancipation Act. **1830s** Reform years. **1837** Victoria inherits the throne. **1848** Chartist uprising. **1867** The first Fenian bombings in England. **1869** Gladstone, religion and land and Ireland. **1880** Home Rule Party holds the balance of power at Westminster. **1886** First Home Rule Bill. **1893** Second Home Rule Bill.	**1763** Britain the leading European nation, and a world power. The rise of the Second British Empire. **1815** The empire of Napoleon is broken up. Peace terms agreed, and a balance of power achieved. **1833** Slavery abolished within the British Empire. **1850** British Empire at its height. Wars in Africa (Ashanti and Zulu) and problems with the Boers in South Africa. **1858** British takeover of India. Colonies of white settlement begin to ask for self-government. Europeans compete for power in Africa. Empires formed by European nations.	**1730 onwards** Expansion of industry from Europe. **1763** The Peace of Paris exchanges land in America, the Caribbean, India and the Far East. **1770** Australia and New Zealand taken by the British. **1776** The American War of Independence. **1789** French Revolution. **1840 onwards** Western influence in Russia, China and Japan. **1848-49** European revolutions. Marx publishes the Communist Manifesto. **1857** Indian War of Independence. **1861** American Civil War. **1865** Italy unified. **1870** Germany unified. **1899-1902** Boer War.
1901 Victoria dies. **1910/11** Crisis of the Lords. **1914** Home Rule Bill passed. First World War. **1920** Extra troops sent to Ireland. **1921** Ulster Parliament opened. **1921** Anglo-Irish Treaty. **1922** IRA attacks in Ulster. **1931** Statute of Westminster. **1936** Edward VIII abdicates. **1939** Britain and the Empire go to War. **1967** Civil Rights campaign in Ulster. Rioting begins. **1972** Direct Rule for Ulster. **1973** Attempted power sharing in Ulster. **1974** Direct Rule reimposed in Ulster. **1985** Anglo-Irish Treaty, Dublin/Westminster.	**1918-20** Peace treaties reshape Europe. The decline of Britain and the rise of America. Britain transfers Empire to Commonwealth. **1936** Fascism in power in Italy, Spain, Germany and Japan. **1945** America leading world nation. Power blocks develop. The Cold War, East and West. Middle Eastern states emerge. **1950 onwards** Dismemberment of the second British Empire and other European empires in the Middle East and Africa.	**1914-18** First World War. **1917** The Russian Revolution. **1933** Hitler rises to power in Germany. Persecution begins. **1939-45** Second World War. **1945** Explosion of nuclear bombs. The Nazi concentration camps opened. **1947** India receives independence. **1949** Chinese Revolution. India becomes a republic.

Index